DIVORCE

REALITY-CHECK

Smart Split Solutions for

Civility, Clarity and Common Sense

By: Jacqueline Harounian, Esq.

New York *'Super Lawyer'*

DIVORCE

Smart Split Solutions for

Civility, Clarity and Common Sense

Reality Check Media
New York

"For a divorce case, that went smoothly."

CONTENTS

PREFACE
(Why I Wrote This Book)

Allow me to introduce myself. My name is Jacqueline Harounian, and for over twenty years, I have practiced divorce and family law in New York (including ten years as a partner) in a top matrimonial law firm in New York. In my day to day life, I go up against the toughest so called "sharks" in the business (and on the rare occasion, I have been called one myself). I have handled extremely complex and contentious divorce trials, cases which last for years and cost more than you could ever imagine, and I have handled quick uncontested divorces and mediation cases that have settled in mere hours.

I wrote this book with the goal of simplifying and demystifying the legal process for my clients and other individuals seeking advice. I want to show you, in the most straightforward way, that a Smart Split is an achievable goal for most couples. I hope to inspire you to envision a legal divorce process that is characterized by Civility, Clarity, and Common Sense – and avoids its unwanted cousins Discord, Drama, and Dysfunction.

As an experienced litigator, I know the divorce system inside and out, and I am more than willing to pull back the curtain and tell you what is really going on in the back rooms where deals are made. I submit to you, dear reader, that I have an expert lens and a needed perspective to guide you along your journey. With that said, I wish I could offer you a guarantee or promise, that this book (or your own reputedly amazing lawyer) can solve your problems and put your mind fully at ease, but I would be lying. The collective words of wisdom and strategies in this book are not foolproof or "one size fits all". **Family law is far from an**

exact science, and even the 'best' alpha lawyer cannot work magic. What I can do is reassure you, by showing you that separation and divorce is a *process*, with a beginning, middle, and end. *You will get through it.* I will show you which aspects of the process are under your control and influence, and which ones are not, no matter how hard you try and how much you spend on legal fees. Although not every topic will apply to your unique situation, my goal is for you to make smarter decisions, starting right this minute, to set the stage for a more secure and healthy future.

INTRODUCTION

Your marriage is irretrievably broken, and life as you know it is unraveling fast. You feel overwhelmed and confused by the well-intentioned (but let's face it, often *clueless*) advice of your friends and family. Does your lawyer's strategy alarm you instead of calm you down? Does the light at the end of the tunnel seem farther and farther away? You are not alone. In fact, you sound like a lot of the men and women who walk into my law office every day. But don't despair. You have come to the right place to find some straight talk about the legal process and the steps you should take to regain your equilibrium and be smarter about your split.

Like most people facing the demise of their marriage, you might feel like your world has turned completely upside down. Uncertainty and unease about the future, and your children's future, may cause you to lose sleep. You may fear being taken for every dime by your vengeful and hell-bent spouse. You may fear losing rights to your most precious assets: your children. You might be intimidated by your spouse, or his lawyer, and maybe even your own lawyer. Still, at a time when your family and financial life are falling apart, it is critical that you take control, and make sound decisions that will affect the rest of your future. But how?

Divorce is a declaration of independence with only two signers.

--Gerald F. Lieberman

Let's break it down. After you get over the emotional hurdles -- a process that is unique to every individual and every relationship -- there are three main legal categories to address,

6

namely: **I. Custody; II. Support;** and **III. Asset Distribution**. Each of these areas must be fully resolved in writing -- by settlement agreement or court order -- before you can move on with your life. Easier said than done to be sure, but take heart. In your hands, you have a GPS to navigate the rocky terrain in the months ahead. You will learn how and why **the high road is the best road**. The organizing tools, lists and 'reality checks' in these pages will help you obtain tangible results and a clearer path. I will coach you with strategies to help you deal with your ex, and provide you with talking points for your meetings with your lawyer. *Pay attention, puhleeze!*

I know that you are at an important crossroads in your life. I encourage you to read this entire book, and be open minded about the possibility of a civilized and uncomplicated break up. Just as I do with my clients, *I am rooting for you* to move on with your life, and to avoid self-destructive and sabotaging behaviors. I urge you to avoid a victim mentality, especially because all that it will get you is an invite to an everlasting 'pity party'. (**Author's Note**: This book is not going to change your life. You have to do that on your own.)

My first objective for you? To calm you and encourage you to think rationally, not emotionally, about your divorce. To begin and strengthen habits of successful financial planning and smooth co-parenting (even when your ex does not necessarily cooperate). Your new mantra starting today? Repeat The Three C's after me: **Civility, Clarity, Common sense.** If, on the other hand, you are feeling angry and vindictive, go find a "shark" lawyer to lead you into Armageddon (and empty your pockets), because *this book is not for you*.

Are you willing to accept some tough love from an expert that has helped thousands of clients move forward with their lives? If so, keep reading!

1.

FIRST THINGS FIRST

"How are you?"

Broken. Useless. Alone. Clueless. Confused. Betrayed. Fragile. On the verge of tears. Depressed. Anxious. About to break down. Really. Give up. Pathetic. Annoying. I'm just a burden. Distant. Lonely. Bitter. Heartbroken. Lonely. Rejected. Crushed. I feel like I'm going to just fall apart at any moment. Empty. Defeated. Never good enough.

Fine.

1

DEALING WITH THE EMOTIONAL FALLOUT

Do you know the definition of a dysfunctional marriage? The answer might surprise you. *A dysfunctional marriage* is *any marriage with more than one person in it.* Every relationship is dysfunctional in its own way, as I can personally attest after 25+ years of matrimony. There is no perfect marriage, just as there are no perfect people in a marriage. The strengths and flaws that make every individual unique are the same factors that make every relationship different from another.

> *Life becomes easier when you learn to accept an apology you never got.*
>
> -- Robert Bravit

From the outset, I want to make one thing clear: I am not here to give anyone ideas about ending their marriage, nor should any reputable divorce professional do that. The truth is, there is no right or wrong when it comes to marriage[1]. **"For better or worse"** means something different for every man and every woman, and every

---

[1] The only exception to this is if you or your children are in danger – in which case you must refer to the last page of this chapter **"What To Do if You Are In A Dangerous Relationship".**

> *The only thing more unthinkable than leaving was staying; the only thing more impossible than staying was leaving.*
> -- Elizabeth Gilbert

individual has their personal bottom line. In my practice, I have encountered people from different cultures, religions, socioeconomic backgrounds and geographic locales, all of whom have a unique threshold of what constitutes "the last straw" of marital misconduct or personal unhappiness. As far as I am concerned, the only **absolute deal breakers** in a marriage are situations of domestic abuse, or where you or your child's personal health or safety is at risk.

STAY OR GO?

I am going to go out on a limb and assume that you are feeling some ambivalence about your decision. You might have your own good reasons for staying in a mediocre or unfulfilling marriage and that is okay. Your decision to forgive a cheating spouse should be your decision, and no one else's. Perhaps you are dealing with your own mid-life crisis, or your spouse is dealing with hers. Personally, I believe that marriage is for the long haul, and a relationship can weather some pretty ugly and even ruinous times without a complete breakdown. In many marriages, years of resentment and feeling unappreciated by a spouse can build up to tsunami levels, and failure to effectively communicate is often the culprit. **Don't make a permanent decision based upon a**

> *Something comes to an end, and something new is born. Your world falls apart, and you are forced to create a new one.*
> -- Donna Karan

temporary emotion. Thus, the first question you should ask yourself is: *Can my relationship be saved?* Some of the best relationships alternate between thunderstorms and sunshine. Others survive for decades with a steady dull overcast sky. If you believe that the relationship can be repaired or improved, and your spouse is on board, then put your collective energies towards that outcome. Initiate marriage counselling with your spouse as soon as possible, and give it 100%. You may just find the silver lining in the clouds.

FIND YOUR TRUTH

If you are ambivalent, it's okay to wait a little while and see if the relationship improves. Take things slowly, but don't live in denial and shame. Recognize that some relationships (and some people) are beyond repair. Sometimes you are faced with a choice: *Do I save the marriage, or my dignity?* Your life might appear to be smooth sailing on the outside, but if you know it's not, seek out the

> *Problems are the knots between pearls.*
> --Dr. Joy Browne

source of the problem. Make changes, starting with yourself. But whether you stay in your marriage or go, make the decision because it is the right decision for you and your children. If a bad marriage or relationship is weighing you down 24/7, if it is making you crazy, miserable, or you are in emotional pain, do something about it. **Take steps to fix it.** Don't tough it out on your own, because there is no shame in calling for backup when you need it. Don't be afraid to change or to challenge the status quo.

TAKE THE TIME TO HEAL

Just as every individual and every relationship is unique, so is every process of separation and divorce. As many struggling couples experience, the end of a marriage is "shock and awe" painful. In fact, dealing with separation and divorce is one of the most challenging emotional crises a man or woman can experience. Even if your marriage was a very short one, or even if you are the one initiating the break up, there can be an overwhelming sense of loss and failure, among a quagmire of intensely negative feelings: betrayal, loneliness, depression, guilt, sorrow, resentment, shame of failure, and anger. For most, there is the angst and dread of facing an uncertain future. Each person deals with the emotional whiplash in their own way and with their own timeline. There is no **right or wrong** way to process the emotional fallout; there are no rules or playbook for how to recover from a divorce. No question, expressing your unfurling hurt and grief is part of the healing process. However, at some point, for your own psychological health and that of your children, you need to move past the fiery emotional stage. In my experience, allowing some time and distance to pass will help you see the

> *Divorce is the psychological equivalent of a triple coronary bypass.*
> -- Mary Kay Blakely

> *If I got locked away, and we lost it all today...if I showed you my flaws, if I couldn't be strong... Tell me honestly, would you still love me the same?*
> -- **Adam Levine**

12

situation more clearly, and to remove yourself from the emotional eye of the storm. After several weeks, if you are still paralyzed with intensely negative feelings, or held captive by unresolved anger and unable to move forward, I advise you to get professional help.

As an experienced divorce attorney, take my word that there is also a critical *strategic* reason to let go of radioactive emotions, and here it is: **If you are still beset with feelings of fear and loathing, when you retain an attorney, I can predict the following trifecta of bad news:**

1. Your divorce case will take longer;

2. It will cost more;

3.   It will be a more negative process that could adversely affect you and your children for the rest of your life.

According to Aristotle, "the law is reason free from passion". However, he most definitely was not referring to the field of matrimonial law, where feelings of passion (i.e. love/hate) are intertwined in virtually every aspect of the process.   In the divorce realm, emotions rule logic and feelings prevail over facts. How does this relate to your case? Simply put, you will not be able to effectively focus on short term decisions and long term economic goals if high-octane emotions are controlling you. If you are still furious, or feeling like a victim of your spouse's betrayal, my best advice to you in the early days and weeks of your situation is to slow down your decision making, and find the time to talk to a trusted friend or therapist about what course of action (if any) is in your best interest.

At our law firm, our team of lawyers personally meets with dozens of prospective clients each month. While many of these clients have already processed the initial emotional fallout of their separation -- many have not. It is easy to spot the

clients that are still reeling from their recent breakup. At our

first meeting, they are often in the early stages of mourning,

and even shock.   Part of my initial assessment of a case in

Divorce is probably as painful as death.
-- William Shatner

the early stages is referring clients to mental health professionals. I may steer a client towards

individual or family therapy, or make suggestions for marriage counseling. Therapy may reveal

underlying psychological issues that the client needs to work on, leading to a decision not to

end the marriage, or to delay the decision for a few months, if not longer. Sometimes the

conflict in the marriage is caused by a breakdown in communication due to extraordinary life

stressors. For example, two working parents might be dealing with a drug addicted teenager,

or a child recently diagnosed with ADHD.   Stressed out parents who are not on the same page

about parenting decisions often point fingers at one another, and the 'blame game' causes

them to fight openly in the presence of their children.

The Bottom Line: When fighting, threats and even physical conflict become the default

mode of interaction over a period of weeks, months or even years, it is common for one or both

parties to acknowledge that a separation is the next logical step, to end the strife.   This brings

me to the **Number One Rule of Separation and Divorce,** which you will find on the next page,

and you should ignore at your own peril:

THE. NUMBER. ONE. RULE.

No matter what your spouse is promising you
in return, or why you think it is a good
idea, you should not move out of the marital
residence, even temporarily, until after you
consult with a lawyer.

In most jurisdictions, moving out for even a
few days can have an impact on the issues of
custody, support, and even access rights to
your residence. For more tips to keep you
steady and help you get through the early days
of your separation and divorce process,
check out the lists on the next pages.

TOP 5 TIPS TO KEEP YOURSELF STEADY AND MAINTAIN EQUILIBRIUM DURING YOUR DIVORCE

#1   *If you have children, put their needs first. Always remember, they didn't ask for this.*

#2   *Plan to remain in your current residence for at least one year, especially if you have children. Don't make impulsive decisions about moving or selling your home without carefully considering all available options.*

#3   *Don't quit or change jobs. Your job is your financial lifeline, especially if you need medical benefits. Despite the emotional havoc you might be feeling, now is the time to maintain your career, not jeopardize it.*

#4   *Don't cash in investment accounts or retirement accounts, or make any rash financial decisions without consulting with your lawyer.*

#5   *Don't start a serious romantic relationship for at least six months. Don't introduce any paramours to your children for at least one year.*

REMEMBER, THE SKY IS NOT FALLING. THIS IS JUST A TEMPORARY STAGE IN YOUR LIFE, NOT YOUR WHOLE LIFE.

CO-PARENTING STRATEGIES:
Taking the "High Road" and Avoiding Drama

1.   **Conflict in the household**, whether it takes the form of a silent cold war, threats, or screaming matches, is toxic to all involved, especially children. Don't fool yourself into thinking that your children aren't affected. You will need every ounce of parenting skills you have to weather the storm ahead. *Make the decision today to be civil to your spouse at all times*. Fake it til you make it. Smile and be polite through gritted teeth if that's what it takes. Dial down the drama whenever you have the opportunity to do so (even when you are screaming on the inside.) This will start the habit of co-parenting and respectful communication, and it will set the stage for a divorce process that is less contentious. **The Lesson: Although this chapter of your life is unscripted, the decision to take the high road starts here.** Consider this Ground Zero for your new reality.

2.   Words are weapons. Don't denigrate your spouse or his family or use inflammatory verbiage. In general, **try not to burn bridges** between you and other people in your children's lives, including ex-in laws. Resist the script that tells you that your divorce must be a melodrama with you and your spouse in enemy camps. **Make it a priority to maintain positive relationships** for the sake of your children and good karma. Even if you and your spouse are no longer living as husband and wife, you are still your children's father and mother. If there has been a decision to separate, but you are still living together, you must make the

effort to transition your mind set from that of spouses, to that of co-parents and roommates. If possible, move to a separate bedroom or area in the house. Do whatever it takes to avoid adult discussions and fighting in front (or within earshot)

You can't underestimate how traumatic divorce is for the children.
--Isla Fisher

of your children. Make it a priority above all else to shield your children from the acrimony as much as possible. A lot of the damage that is done to children during separation and divorce occurs when they are front row and center to name calling, threats and even violence in the final weeks and months before the actual separation.

3.   Co-parenting requires discipline, self-control and most of all, a shared goal of putting your children's interests first. **Pay attention** to your children's feelings, behavior, academic performance, online activities and friendships. Strive to maintain cordial communication with your spouse regarding your children's needs. These include arrangements for carpools, homework, and medical appointments. If you are having difficulty with conversations with your spouse, utilize email and text to communicate as much as possible. (Avoid snarky or sarcastic language. Avoid passive aggressive communication and respond timely to requests from your spouse about the children and day to day financial matters.) With practice and the passage of time, bit by bit and day by day, you will learn to **separate your feelings towards your spouse** from your responsibilities as a co-parent, and build trust.

4.   If you and your spouse have a civil relationship and can communicate productively, discuss ground rules for the early days and weeks of your separation. Write up some terms, but don't sign anything without consulting with a lawyer. If you and your spouse

can reach an understanding about how pay the bills in the house, and how to manage the

children's needs, activities, schedule, etc., you will **eliminate a lot of the sources of tension and**

conflict in the household during the first days and weeks. Try to maintain the status quo as

best you can. (If you already have a lawyer, you can ask your lawyer to confirm details by

letter. This will ensure that there are no misunderstandings in the early stages of the case.)

5. Do you need another compelling reason to be on your very best behavior while

you are going through a divorce? *Well, tah-dah! Here it is.* If you

act out or lash out in front of your spouse, you might be confronted

with evidence of your misconduct that will be used against you later

on. Today's **technology is both powerful and dangerous,** especially

when there is adrenaline in your blood and the smell of revenge is

If you are going through hell, keep going.
-- Winston Churchill

in the air. Assume you are being taped by your spouse 24/7 and act accordingly. Resist the

powerful urge to pour salt on old wounds. Here's a no brainer: refrain from calling your STBX[2]

a "deadbeat" or "loser" (or worse) to his face (However, it is perfectly ok to whisper it to

yourself.) Be cordial in all your texts and emails. Avoid rants on Facebook or knee jerk text

wars. All of these can and will be used against you, and will ramp up the conflict. Don't

underestimate your spouse, and don't give his lawyer ammunition to use in a character

assassination against you. (See Chapter 6, "How to Lose Custody in 7 Easy Steps", for more tips

on how foolish and self-destructive behavior can and will affect your custody rights.)

---

[2] STBX = Soon to be Ex

6.   Begin the process of asking for lawyer referrals and make a list.   But before you hire a lawyer, spend some time with a trusted friend or family member, a coworker or clergy member, who will listen to you, and give you some guidance. If you feel weighed down emotionally, overwhelmed or depressed, write your thoughts in a journal. **Try to find some clarity** about what you are dealing with in your relationship and what you want from life in the years ahead. Your hopes and goals for the future will likely change now that the love of your life, i.e. your 'soulmate', is now referred to as 'the defendant'. Find a therapist who can help you develop coping strategies and give you perspective to better deal with this new uncharted territory of life's journey. In the meantime, resist the urge to lay blame on other people in your life, and **leave the past in the past.**

> *Rock bottom became the solid foundation on which I rebuilt my life.*
> - J.K. Rowling

AVOIDING A VICTIMOLOGY NARRATIVE

When you discuss your divorce with the other people in your life (including your mom, Facebook friends, and coworkers) do you use the language of victimology and martyrdom? Is your personal narrative one that lays the blame on everyone around you (including your ex, your parents, and/or your boss)? Victimology is the science of feeling good about feeling bad. By blaming others, you let yourself off the hook to find solutions and take action to improve your life. Focusing on victimhood and negative outcomes creates a self-fulfilling prophecy. 'Fess up. Are you a victimologist? Or do you hold yourself accountable for your actions, your choices, and your role in relationships? By taking appropriate responsibility for your life, starting today, you lay the groundwork for future growth, and a brighter future.

WHAT TO DO IF YOU ARE IN A *DANGEROUS* RELATIONSHIP

Know this: There is nothing more important than keeping yourself and your children out of harm's way.

1. Do not hesitate to call "911" or go to the police anytime you are threatened or assaulted. Your local police are trained to deal with domestic violence. The police report is proof that you reported violence by your abuser.

2. Find a therapist, counselor, or support group. There are many agencies that provide support for victims at low cost or no cost. If there are children in the household, enroll the children in therapy and speak to the school psychologist.

3. Keep a journal detailing any incidents that occur, including date and time, location, photographs, copies of texts, and names of witnesses.

4. Take photographs of your injuries and property damage and keep the photos in a very safe place (not stored on your phone). Gather some cash, your passport and children's passports and keep these in a safe place in the event of a true emergency.

5. If your children are assaulted, or they witness any abuse or violence in the household, call Child Protective Services. They will investigate immediately, and keep your information confidential.

6. Go to Family Court to obtain an order of protection against your spouse. In most cases, you do not need an attorney to obtain one. There are several types of orders including a limited order, stay away order, removal of weapons in the household, and prohibitions from use of alcohol and drugs in the household.

7. If you have questions about separation, divorce, custody or financial support, contact a local family law attorney for a confidential consultation. Go to Avvo.com or Lawyers.com to find attorneys, many of whom do not charge for the initial consultation.

2.

GET ORGANIZED

2

GET ORGANIZED *BEFORE* YOU HIRE A LAWYER

In the preceding chapter, I stressed the importance of letting the emotional

temperature cool in your relationship before you proceed with your case. In other words, if the

break up is fresh, and the conflict has the potential to take on the plot of a Greek tragedy, **don't**

strike when the iron is HOT. To do otherwise ensures a volatile start to your divorce, and

increases the chance that simple issues will escalate throughout the case.

MOVING FROM PANIC TO PLANNING

Once you have steered past the emotional obstacles that might cloud your rational

decision making and put you into "reaction mode", you are ready to tackle the process of

divorce planning and organization. Every battle, even a friendly one, requires preparation. You

need to do your homework. If you have the means and find the task of getting organized too

overwhelming, this would be a good time to consult with a divorce financial planner, or other

divorce coach. For the rest of you who are willing to take this on personally, you might find that marshalling all of the financial nuts and bolts of your life gives you a sense of calm and control over the divorce process. Give it a shot! You have nothing to lose and a lot to gain, as I will explain in this chapter.

This divorce planning "homework" will take several days, if not weeks, depending on the complexity of the issues in your case. As with any project, it is helpful to break it down into smaller, manageable steps. Be assured that although the planning stage can be time consuming, the huge cost-saving and organizational benefits will be apparent later on when you begin working with your attorney and other professionals involved in your case. Even more importantly, you can "hit the ground running" when you are ready to move ahead with your case. Are you ready to begin? **Let's get started!**

HERE ARE THE FIVE STEPS TO
THE DIVORCE PLANNING MASTER LIST

➡	STEP 1:	Your Wish List and Goals
➡	STEP 2:	Background Facts
➡	STEP 3:	Financial Issues Checklist
➡	STEP 4:	Divorce Planning and Action List
➡	STEP 5:	Assembling your Professional Dream Team

As you can see, The Master List is not just about organizing your finances. It is a tool to help you clarify your goals and identify potential issues. If you start your case with these steps, you have a much better chance of getting to the finish line with maximum results and minimal time, expense, and negative karma.

STEP 1: *Your Wish List*

Time Commitment: 1-2 hours

When I start working with my clients, one of the first things I ask them to do is come up with a set of goals – both short term (within the next 1 to 6 months) and long term (6 months to one year or longer).   Then I take inventory. What are they looking for? How do they envision the next chapter in their life? What do their children need?   I ask them to think in terms of a "wish list" with the understanding that not all of their goals will be achievable, or even legally advisable. But it is a starting point for them to brain storm about the outcome they desire, and most importantly to **prioritize their goals**.

Once I know what their objectives are, I can make an initial 'reality check' assessment. Are their goals realistic? Are they asking for too much? Are they shortchanging themselves? Would a postnuptial agreement or referral to a mental health counselor better suit their immediate needs?   As the case unfolds over the course of the next few weeks and months, I will confer with opposing counsel and my client. If the parties are cooperating with their counsel, and focused on resolving issues, the terms of a potential settlement will begin to take shape (See Chapter 5 for tips on a Smart Split). At that point, I will have another conversation with my client about the wish list, with a view towards creating a legal strategy. **Which goals are they willing to bend on? Which items on the list are deal breakers? What risks are presented if there is an impasse in negotiations and we have to go to court? Is the client**

comfortable with those risks? As you work together with your lawyer and other professionals, it is never too early to start focusing on the finish line, i.e. terms for settlement and the ultimate resolution of your case.

By writing down your personal and financial fears and fantasies in black and white, you force yourself into awareness. This will create clarity in your mind regarding your future goals and desires. Ideally, you will begin identifying and moving forward with your short term and long term priorities (for the next few weeks and months, the next year, and the next five years.)

SOME EXAMPLES OF GOALS

- *I want primary residential custody of our children.*

- *I need $2500 per month in support so that I can stay in this house until our youngest child graduates high school.*

- *I received an inheritance from my father, and I want to make sure that I protect that money from claims by my spouse.*

- *I am willing to split all joint assets equally.*

- *I want to build up a better credit score.*

- *I will not agree to contribute to my spouse's credit card debt.*

HOW TO CREATE YOUR WISH LIST

Find a quiet hour or two and sit down with a notebook, or your laptop[3]. If it will help you clarify your thoughts and objectives, have a candid discussion with a friend or therapist. Make a list of short term goals and desired long term outcomes and then write a sentence or two for each goal. Remember, this is not a final list and it is for your eyes only. You can add to and amend this list periodically as you move forward. The tools on the next few pages will help.

As you formulate your list, you should also generate some **notes and questions** to ask your attorney, such as: What are the possible outcomes (or range of outcomes)? Is my goal realistic? What proof do I need to achieve this goal? What documents do I need to review before I decide? **What costs are anticipated for legal and expert fees?** Try to visualize your life post separation and ask yourself: What is most important to me? Which items can I let go of?

---

[3] My recommendation? Purchase a 3 ring binder with pocket folders. Have tabs for each part of the Master List. Use the binder to store receipts, your parenting schedule and calendar, and essential financial and legal documents. You can write down questions for your next meeting with your lawyer, and store copies of important photos, emails, texts that might be needed as evidence later on. Needless to say, keep your notebook in a very safe place. For a more secure, high tech option, scan the documents and store them on a flash drive, your smart phone, or personal laptop. The added benefit of the paperless option is that the documents can then be scanned and emailed to your lawyer, which will save time and money.

ISSUE:	Wish List / Goals:	Notes /Questions:
Emergency / Urgent Custody Concerns		
Child Custody Schedule		
Child Support		
Child Care / Activities		
The Marital Residence		
Spousal Support		
Other Short Term Goals		
Emergency / Urgent Financial Concerns		
Medical Insurance		

Life Insurance		
Division of Assets		
Division of Debts		
Separate Property Issues		
Long Term Goals		

MAKING A CUSTODY SCHEDULE

SUNDAY	MONDAY	TUESDAY	WEDNESDAY	THURSDAY	FRIDAY	SATURDAY

If you and your spouse have minor children, your next task is to fill in the monthly calendar that appears above. Consider you work schedule, your spouse's schedule and the children's schedule. Fill in the weekdays and weekends with "M" for Mother and "F" for Father. **What basic schedule do you propose for custody?** Alternating weekends with each parent? Two evenings each week after school? Be sure to keep your children's regular activities in mind, as well as pick up times from religious school, day care, or soccer practice. Understand that your spouse might have very different ideas about a parenting schedule. Keep an open mind, and realize that no schedule is "written in stone". Flexibility and reciprocity between co-parents are key to raising well-adjusted children, and maintaining adult sanity.

Next, make a **LIST OF HOLIDAYS** (secular and religious), birthdays and school recess periods that you celebrate. Consult with the school calendar to see which days your children will be home. Give some thought as to how these days might be shared or alternated with your spouse from year to year.

_____   _____

_____   _____

_____   _____

_____   _____

Finally, give some thought to **DECISION MAKING REGARDING LEGAL CUSTODY ISSUES.** Do you and your ex communicate well regarding the children's religious upbringing, medical treatment and academic interests? These are areas where parents must consult with each other and reach agreement. If there are problems or major decisions to be made, parents must agree on how to address these.

MEDICAL: _____

ACADEMIC: _____

RELIGIOUS: _____

ACTIVITIES: _____

SPECIAL NEEDS:_____

TRAVEL: _____

STEP 2: Background Facts

Time Commitment: 2 hours

The next step is to type up a narrative summary of your relationship with your spouse, starting with your courtship and wedding day, and continuing all the way up to the present. Include as many details as possible, and put each event in chronological order. Include dates and places regarding the births of your children and your job history. Include places where you have lived, and major milestones such as the purchase of your house (including mortgage and refinance details), home renovations and how these were paid for, inheritances, major gifts, businesses opened or closed, and any partnerships. Include details regarding career development, licenses and degrees obtained, unemployment, bankruptcies, tax issues, debts, monies borrowed from family or elsewhere. Write up details about your children's needs: medical, academic, extracurricular activities, special needs, child care, camp, tutors. Describe the contributions and sacrifices both you and your spouse have made during the marriage, and add details regarding your religious ceremony, prenuptial agreement or religious contracts, if these apply to your case.

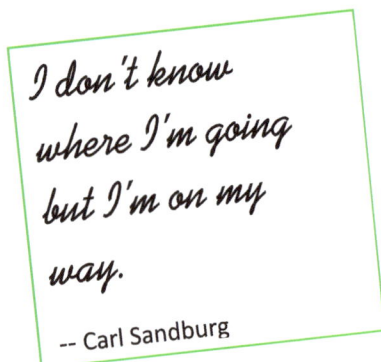

> *I don't know where I'm going but I'm on my way.*
> -- Carl Sandburg

The background narrative will be tremendously helpful in your case because it will provide factual context well beyond what can be covered in a face to face meeting with your attorney or mediator. Email the document to your lawyer, which will make it very easy (and less costly) for your lawyer to copy and paste the information into legal documents if necessary.

STEP 3: *Financial Issues Checklist*

Time Commitment: 1 – 3 hours

If your case is like most others, the lion's share of the negotiations will deal with financial issues. This breaks down into two main areas of "wheeling and dealing":

1. **Support Issues** (which are based on income and expenses), and

2. **Asset / Debt Distribution Issues** (which are based on assets and debts).

In order for these two categories to be fully analyzed by your attorney and other experts involved in your case, you will need to identify all of the financial factors in your case. The Step 3 Financial Issues Checklist is designed to give you a heads up and a head start before you sit down with your lawyer.

SUPPORT issues are present in those cases where: a) there are minor children of the marriage, or b) there is enough disparity between the income of the parties to give rise to a spousal support claim. The laws applicable to child support and spousal support vary in every state, so check with your lawyer to find out more about your support entitlements or obligations.

ASSET / DEBT DISTRIBUTION issues are found in virtually every marriage of one year duration or longer[4]. Most states follow guidelines for "community property" or "equitable

---

[4] I have handled several divorces for marriages that regrettably lasted only a few months. During divorce negotiations, the only issue to be resolved was the distribution of wedding gifts and/or the debt related to the wedding reception and/or honeymoon.

distribution" which hold that assets acquired during the marriage are to be shared between the parties. The same goes for debts.

The financial issues in your divorce case can be described as **SIMPLE** if your income and assets are relatively easy to inventory, document, and appraise (i.e. cars, bank accounts, real estate, and retirement accounts).   If you or your spouse's income and assets are hidden, unreported, or difficult to document (i.e. businesses, partnerships, cash, stock options), then your financial issues can be described as **COMPLEX.**

TO IDENTIFY ALL OF THE FINANCIAL ISSUES IN YOUR CASE, GATHER THE FOLLOWING:

➡ **INCOME** - a list of all income sources for you and all members of your household.

➡ **EXPENSES** - a list of every recurring and non-recurring expense for you and members of your household.

➡ **ASSETS** - a one page listing of you and your spouse's assets, and their approximate current value.

➡ **DEBTS** – a one page summary of the debts and liabilities incurred during the marriage.

INCOME AND EXPENSES

For **INCOME**, your starting point is your tax return and paystub. This includes W-2 income, 1099 income, pension income, Social Security and disability income, royalties, rental income from investment property, interest and dividends. Employment benefits and tax write offs (if you own a business) may also be considered income.

For **EXPENSES**, look carefully at your household budget; who pays what?   What does it cost to run your household, and pay the bills for school, child care, and insurance? Look at your online banking, checkbook, and credit cards to make sure you don't forget recurring and non-recurring expenses for yourself and members of your household.   The more organized you are about capturing the details related to your household and family expenses, the more information your lawyer will have to present to opposing counsel, or to the court if necessary, in connection with your support claim. So track down every receipt for every single expense, and record these in a journal or on an Excel spreadsheet.

ASSETS AND DEBTS

For **ASSETS**, include bank accounts, real property, cars, investments, personal property and artwork. Besides equity in a marital home, the largest asset is usually retirement assets. These include pensions, IRAs, annuities, 401k, 403b. Other assets to be considered include military pensions, stock options, bonuses, deferred compensation, time shares, life insurance, savings bonds, and college savings accounts. For each asset, note when each asset was acquired, the approximate purchase price of each, and its estimated current value.

For **DEBTS**, include credit card debts, mortgage debts, HELOC, student loans, personal loans, car leases, pension loans, and tax liabilities.

THE BASIC PROCESS TO ANALYZE MARITAL ASSETS

➡ ONE: Identify the asset.

➡ TWO: Classify the asset as a marital asset or separate asset

➡ THREE: Document or appraise the asset to determine its value.

➡ FOUR: Distribute the asset between the parties.

ASSETS	Marital or Separate?	Value

STEP 4: *Divorce Planning and Action List*

Time Commitment: 2 days to 2 weeks

	Action Item	✔
→	Order a copy of your credit report. The three credit reporting agencies are Equifax: 1-888-202-4025, TransUnion: 1-800-888-4213, and Experian: 1-888-397-3742	
→	Obtain copies of tax returns (at least five years). If you do not have access to copies, then go online to IRS.gov (Form 4506) to order copies at no charge. While you are on the IRS website, obtain a copy of IRS Publication 504 for Divorced Couples.	
→	Go online to SSA.gov to find out current information regarding your Social Security benefits. The same website has very useful information regarding your retirement benefits after divorce.	
→	Don't sign any loan or HELOC documents or contracts, or listing agreements for the marital residence or other real property.	
→	Don't sign a joint tax return without consulting first with your own lawyer or accountant.	
→	Obtain copies of W-2 statements, recent paystubs and 1099 for yourself and your spouse.	

➡	If you have received a gift or inheritance during your marriage, including real property, do not deposit it into a joint account, or add your spouse's name to the asset. Keep very careful records, and consult with a lawyer to obtain legal advice on how to protect this asset during a divorce.	
➡	Change passwords for all of your home utility accounts, online banking and social media accounts. If you share a home computer with your spouse, be careful of any information that might be on the computer that can be used against you, including spyware.	
➡	Gather copies of all bank statements and check registers for you and your spouse. Make a list of all closed accounts. Some of this information can be obtained from your tax returns.	
➡	Obtain a credit card in your own name. Keep payments current. If you are concerned about your spouse's spending on a joint credit card, you can freeze the spending limit on the card, or cancel the card. You can do the same for a line of credit, bank overdraft account, or HELOC.	
➡	Obtain copies of all mortgage documents and loan applications.	
➡	Save as much money as you can in a separate bank account in your name to create an emergency fund (to cover at least 3 months of your basic expenses.) If necessary, suspend payments for unnecessary luxuries, including allowance payments to adult children.	
➡	Secure valuable including jewelry, passports (including your children's passports) and diplomas at the home of a friend or trusted family member.	

➡	If you have a joint bank account, and you think your spouse might cut you off financially when he or she finds out about the divorce, take exactly half of the balance of funds in the account and deposit it into a separate bank account.	
➡	Photograph and videotape the contents of your home safe, safe deposit box, jewelry, artwork, and home furnishings.	
➡	Keep current on medical and dental appointments. If you do not have your own health insurance, keep in mind that your coverage might end when the divorce is finalized.	
➡	Consult with your own separate accountant to review joint tax returns, especially if your spouse has a business or partnership.	
➡	Make sure that your car is in good running order. Trade in your car for a cheaper one, or lease a car to reduce expenses.	
➡	Keep an eye on your spouse's incoming mail, especially investments, tax documents, retirement assets and credit cards. Take down information regarding account numbers and return addresses.	
➡	Have regular repairs made to the marital residence so that it doesn't fall into disrepair during the divorce proceedings. Keep a file regarding any insurance claims or weather damage.	

STEP 5: *Assembling Your Professional "Dream Team"*

Although this is the last step of planning, it should not be overlooked. Unless you have a very simple case, there will likely be a number of professional experts that play a role in your case. The list below is just a starting point for discussions with your lawyer, and I have broken it down into two main categories: 1. Non-Financial / Custody Experts and 2. Financial Experts. The use of one or more professional financial experts depends on the types of assets in your case, and whether the parties can agree on valuation of these assets. When assets or income are hidden, it will be almost impossible for your attorney to guide you unless the necessary documentation is obtained and analyzed. Keep in mind, locating and investigating assets adds significantly to the price tag of the process.

Consider your attorney the general contractor in charge of your case, with sub-contractors, i.e. court appointed or other experts, as listed below.

NON-FINANCIAL / CUSTODY EXPERTS

- Therapist (for yourself and/or children). Use in network providers whenever possible to keep costs down.

- Private Investigator (for custody and financial issues)

- Forensic Expert to retrieve electronic data and computer data

- Forensic Custody Evaluators

- Employment Counselor

- Custody Mediator

- o   Parent Coordinator

- o   Life Coach or Divorce Consultant

FINANCIAL EXPERTS

- o   Accountant (to review your tax returns and advise you of the tax impact of support and division of assets, including retirement assets)

- o   Forensic accountant to value a business, partnership, profit sharing or stock options;

- o   Life Insurance Broker

- o   Certified Divorce Financial Planner (CDFP)

- o   Health Insurance Broker

- o   College Savings Plan Advisor

- o   Investment Advisor / Financial Planner

- o   Pension Plan Actuary

- o   Real estate Broker

- o   Real estate Appraiser

- o   Appraiser for artwork, cars or boat

- o   Mortgage Broker

3.

A CAUTIONARY TALE

3

A CAUTIONARY TALE:
Avoiding a
"War of the Roses"

After twenty years as a divorce lawyer, I am firmly convinced that the 1989 movie "War of the Roses" (starring Kathleen Turner and Michael Douglas) should be required viewing for two groups: couples contemplating marriage and couples contemplating divorce. If you are ever tempted to give in to "the low road" of revenge and retaliation against your spouse, I urge you to download this Hollywood satire on Netflix and watch it today.   A "war of the roses" is a term of art among matrimonial attorneys. Indeed, it is a phrase that is pervasive throughout American culture. It is essentially the worst case scenario that many people envision when they hear of a marital break-up with major drama, unreasonable demands and aggressive lawyering.

The movie displays how a seemingly idyllic romance followed by a seemingly perfect marriage can morph over time into obsessive hatred. It shows how a once adoring spouse can become your worst enemy and fiercest competitor.   Oliver and Barbara Rose seem to have achieved the ultimate American dream, complete with 'happily ever after'. Oliver is a handsome and successful lawyer; Barbara is a gorgeous domestic goddess, raising two children, a girl and a boy. Their incredible house is the stuff of dreams, decorated to the hilt, with a wine cellar and wood paneled library for him, and walk in shoe closets and a designer kitchen for her. Now fast forward a few years. The house is still a showpiece. The kids are spoiled, but grown up and about to leave the nest. But

Anyone who's been through a divorce will tell you that at one point, they've thought of murder. The line between thinking murder and doing murder isn't that major.
--Oliver Stone

Barbara is unfulfilled and seething with anger, searching for her own identity after seventeen years as a homemaker. Oliver is at the pinnacle of his career, working long hours and utterly clueless about the state of his relationship. The gorgeous house is only a facade, hiding a marriage in deep trouble.

When Barbara requests a divorce, her husband is completely blindsided. The announcement ends with her vow to hire the best divorce attorney *his money* can buy. Oliver (like many defendants in my practice), for one reason or another, is not ready to accept that his marriage is over. He thinks that if he stands his ground and hangs in there, a reconciliation might occur. (In my experience, actual reconciliation occurs less than 5% of the time.) Oliver is certainly not going to move out of *his house*. Meanwhile, as the "breadwinner" of the family, Oliver is likely to pay for most, if not all of the litigation costs, including both lawyers, as well as 100% of the expenses for the house, the children, and his soon to be ex-wife. Most breadwinners cannot tolerate this scenario for very long.

Nothing is so unproductive as the law. It is expensive whether you win or lose.
-- Gilbert Parker

It's time to fasten your seat belt. The plot unfolds: we watch the Rose divorce go "nuclear" and there is no turning back. Barbara destroys her husband's priceless figurine collection. Oliver saws the heels off his wife's designer shoes. He then urinates in her soup (sabotaging her new catering business) and destroys her fancy designer kitchen. Barbara locks him the sauna, where he nearly dies. Then she crashes her massive SUV into Oliver's beloved vintage convertible, with him still behind the wheel. (Barbara, ostensibly a member of the "weaker sex", gives as good as she gets.) Unbelievably, despite the utter mayhem depicted in the movie, both parties are permitted to reside together in the house until the final decree of divorce. (In a real case, one of the parties, most likely the husband, would be served with an order of protection and forced to vacate the residence, especially because there are children present witnessing the violence.)

Misery is the company of lawsuits. -- Francois Rabelais

The Roses pay the ultimate price in their divorce by refusing to settle their case, as can be seen at the very dramatic end of the story. (I won't give it away, but it involves Kathleen Turner and Michael Douglas hanging on for dear life from the enormous crystal chandelier high above their foyer.) The Rose divorce is characterized by unresolved anger and discord, which escalates violently with each scene of the movie. Ironically, the gorgeous mansion, which Oliver worked so hard to pay for, and Barbara worked so hard to decorate and entertain in, becomes a war zone. The house is their undoing and the ultimate pawn in the litigation. The retaliatory behavior by both parties is stunningly vindictive.

She cried – and the Judge wiped away her tears with my checkbook. -- Tommy Manville

Danny DeVito, the husband's divorce lawyer, is the film's narrator and the only voice of

reason. As the story unfolds, he reveals the deep truth of every

contested divorce battle. Every divorcing couple has a choice: to

have a War of the Roses, by spitefully and foolishly refusing to

Eye for an eye.
Tooth for a tooth.
- The Bible

resolve any issue, and ignoring legal advice -- or -- by working things out, by letting go, moving

on, by making reasonable concessions, or even being generous to your spouse -- a person you

once loved and with whom you brought children into the world.

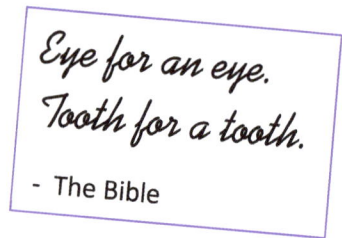

One of the best lines in the movie (and one I often use myself with clients) is when

DeVito says: **"There is no winning -- only degrees of losing."** In other words, the sooner that

the parties can settle their case and move on with their lives, the better off they will be. Parties

who endlessly litigate and who spend a fortune on legal fees, usually need some help putting

things in perspective. When couples are in the last stages of an unhappy relationship, and

emotions are running high, it can be easy to buy into the idea of **divorce as death match.**

(**Author's Note**: Ask yourself: Would you rather promote Peace or War? Take it from a pro –

years down the road, you will reap the many rewards that come from choosing a peaceful

process rather than a war.)

TALES FROM THE FRONT

Below is a list of examples of misconduct and mayhem from actual cases I have handled. (Names and a few details have been changed to protect the less than innocent.)

Sharon retained me to represent her in her divorce after her (triple board certified surgeon) husband assaulted her during a family vacation after she accused him of infidelity. The parties had a 10 year old son. During financial discovery, she viewed her husband's tax returns for the first time. That is when she learned that her husband had other dependents he was supporting: three more children under the age of ten (from two other baby mamas). During a break in the divorce trial, while the husband was testifying on the stand, my client admitted to me that she had a 'one night stand' with her husband only a week ago, but still wanted to proceed with the trial.

Jonathan, married for nearly 20 years and the father of three children, was denied access to parenting time with his children for over three years, despite the fact that he was living in the house right next door to his wife and children the whole time.

My client **Rhonda** was married to a successful lawyer who cheated on her with his paralegal. As part of their quickie settlement agreement less than two months after the affair was discovered, he agreed to walk away from virtually all of the marital assets, including their $3 Million waterfront home with no mortgage.

Lenore and Matthew successfully negotiated all of the issue in their case including custody, support, and division of the major assets. However, the settlement broke down over the final issue: the division of personal property. Both parties wanted a small green jade Buddha statue that they bought together on vacation ten years prior. The litigation over the statue cost each party over $5,000 in attorney fees.

Nicole's husband, John, dumped all of her clothing and personal property into a dumpster at the urging of his new girlfriend. During settlement negotiations, he was forced to pay more than $4,000 to replace the items he threw away.

Isabelle's husband tried to run over the process server with his car, while he was being served with the divorce Summons.

Roxana and Albert were never married. They fought a bitter custody battle over their 12 year old daughter, who suffered from a severe anxiety disorder. Each parent accused the other of being unfit, and the child, caught in the middle, said she wanted to live with both parents. The court appointed psychologist issued a report, which stated that the parents were responsible for the child's psychological issues. The Family Court Judge ordered placement of the child in foster care, which was devastating to the parties. Less than one week later, the parties reached an agreement on 50/50 shared custody and the child was returned to them.

Frank and Mary were married for nearly 35 years and could not reach an agreement about how to divide their marital property or the issue of spousal support. Six months after the case started, during Mary's court ordered deposition in my office conference room, Frank asked if he could have fifteen minutes to talk with her alone, and Mary's lawyer agreed. One hour later, Frank and Mary were still talking. They came out of the conference room and announced that they decided to reconcile.

Lisa and Charlie were married for 15 years. At the time of the separation, they had a wine collection valued by an expert at over $200,000. By the time of trial, most of the wine was "missing", each side claimed they had no idea what happened.

You can't help but feel sympathy [for her] but you know, the solution is to get a divorce. For heaven's sake, if a man is cheating on you, you do what every other woman in the country does. Take him to the cleaners. Take his house, take his car, take his kids, take his respect in the community, and you can make him wish he were dead, but you don't get to kill him."

- Assistant District Attorney Mia Magness, discussing defendant Dr. Clara Harris, who killed her cheating husband.

4.

FINDING THE BEST LEGAL PROCESS FOR YOUR CASE

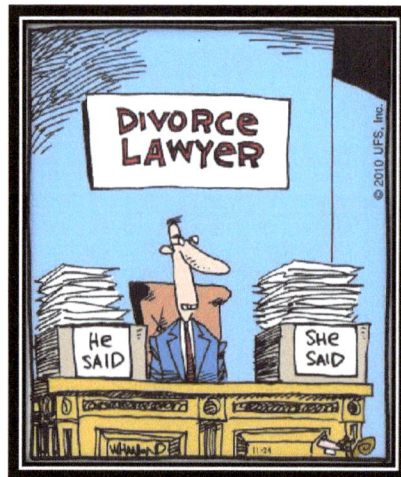

4

FINDING THE BEST
LEGAL PROCESS
FOR YOUR CASE

It goes without saying that you should go to any lengths to avoid an escalated conflict in

your divorce[5]. If you have your goals in mind, and have worked through the other steps of The

Master List in Chapter 2, now it's time to discuss these with a family law professional, lawyer or

mediator. One of the first things that you will have to actually decide, proactively and

preemptively, is what type of process best suits your case.[6]

What motivates many people to run to a lawyer and serve papers is the assumption that

their spouse will make aggressive claims and, as they say, "take them to the cleaners"[7]. But this is

an assumption based on fear. Don't let fear dictate your legal strategy. Don't be the one who fires

the opening salvo in a war of scorched earth litigation. Realize that many cases are successfully

resolved to conclusion by tried-and-true methods of traditional negotiation, not litigation,

especially if both parties make a global resolution a priority and cooperate with each other and

---

[5] If you still aren't convinced, read Chapter 3 again.

[6] Of course, if your spouse has already retained counsel and has served you with divorce
papers, this decision might be out of your hands.

[7] In most cases, it makes no difference who files first, i.e. who is plaintiff and who is defendant.
Exceptions to this rule include domestic violence cases or contested child custody proceedings.

their counsel. **Furthermore, in all likelihood, even if your case goes to court, it will settle well before the trial, as over 95% of cases do.** Before you start your case, be aware that there are five different options for the divorce process, which are represented on the chart below.

I. SIMPLE UNCONTESTED, II. MEDIATION, and **III. COLLABORATIVE LAW.**

IV. TRADITIONAL NEGOTIATION and **V. LITIGATION.**

PROCESS:		COST:	TIME FRAME:	STRESS FACTOR:
I. SIMPLE UNCONTESTED	• Simple cases • Brief marriages • Childless marriages • No assets • Straightforward support issues • Lawyer optional	$	1 week to 1 month	Very Low
II. MEDIATION	• Simple cases • Income and assets are easy to document • Parties communicate well and are ready to compromise. • Parties can work with a neutral mediator as well as have their own attorneys to advise them.	$-$$	2 weeks to 6 months	Low
III. COLLABORATIVE LAW	• Simple to complex custody and/or financial issues. • Each party has a lawyer, and both parties must agree not to litigate.	$$-$$$	6 months to 1 + years	Low to Medium

IV. **TRADITIONAL** **NEGOTIATION**	• Simple to complex custody and/or financial issues. • Each party has their own lawyer. • Usually starts out of court, but may go to litigation if there is an impasse in negotiations or judicial intervention is needed.	$$-$$$	6 months to 1+ years	Low to High
V. **LITIGATION**	• Complex custody and/or financial issues. • Neutral experts required. • Emergency issues must be addressed by judicial intervention. • Each party has a lawyer.	$$$ -$$$$+	1 to 3 years	High

Options I, II and III keep you out of a courtroom altogether. Option IV, Traditional Negotiation, is the most common and versatile process, because you can start out with settlement discussions out of court, but later on obtain judicial intervention if a strategy change is needed. Option V, Litigation, starts out with the filing of an emergency motion in court or other procedure to get a judge assigned to the case. The decision to litigate your divorce case should be made very carefully, and with defined objectives. In the vast majority of cases, litigation should not be your opening strategy, unless there is a compelling circumstance that requires the expertise of a judge. **The divorce processes that are intended to stay out of court (I, II, III, and sometimes IV) are generally quicker, less costly and less adversarial in nature.**

My advice to you: If you are ambivalent about which of the five processes is best for you, do some research asap!

STRAIGHT TALK ABOUT
DIVORCE MEDIATION

As an attorney who is also a mediator, I believe that mediation is a good option for many divorcing couples, especially those with simple financial circumstances, and who mostly agree on the big issues. Mediation is a relatively cordial process, and can save you thousands of dollars in legal fees. In addition, if you choose mediation, you can still opt to have your own attorney advise you and review the agreement before you sign it. If you feel you have a straightforward case, and your spouse will agree to meet with a mediator, then you have nothing to lose. Read the rest of this chapter very carefully, and then give it a try.

However, because I am also an experienced litigator, I have seen my share of egregiously one-sided and unfair mediation agreements. I have counseled clients that are absolutely devastated by regret and the fear of financial ruin because they went through mediation without considering the other options. In those cases, a client's only option may be to go to court and attempt to have the mediation agreement set aside[8]. Here's the thing: Mediation is truly a situation of *caveat emptor*, or buyer beware. There are certain divorce matters that are simply not a good fit for mediation, and most certainly will put you at a significant disadvantage in your case. Before you commit to a process of mediation (or collaborative law) be aware of the

---

[8] A mediation agreement can only be set aside in very limited circumstances, including duress, nondisclosure or fraud. See a lawyer without delay if you believe you have sufficient grounds to seek this relief in court.

pitfalls[9]. Otherwise, you can unwittingly waste a lot of time and money, only to end up having to hire an attorney and start over when the process fails to yield a settlement agreement.

HEADS UP:
4 RED FLAG SCENARIOS

1. You and your spouse cannot communicate.

A successful mediation process hinges on communication, compromise and flexibility between parties that trust each other (at least to some degree). If domestic violence or intimidation are part of your relationship with your spouse, mediation is not for you. If you feel uncomfortable speaking about sensitive financial or custody matters in the presence of your spouse, proceed carefully. If your spouse is domineering, or a bully, or suffers from a personality disorder (i.e. narcissism, borderline, or sociopath), you will be at a distinct disadvantage in your mediation, because your spouse will try to control the process. An experienced divorce mediator can spot these types a mile away, and most will advise you that you would benefit from having your own lawyer to represent you.

2. Unequal playing field / assets are hidden

If you are in the dark about your finances, and your spouse controls all of the financial information related to your marriage, mediation is a risky process for you. If your spouse operates a business or is

---

[9] Just because mediation won't work for your case, this does not mean that your case is going to court. As set forth in the previous chapter, many cases settle without going to court, with each party working with their own lawyer instead of with a neutral mediator. (See IV. Traditional Negotiation.)

involved in a business partnership, and you don't have enough information about it, proceed with caution. There are simply too many unknowns in this scenario, and business owners often employ tax strategies regarding their income and debts that are not immediately apparent on tax returns or balance sheets. If there are complex assets in your case, don't make a deal without the benefit of your own legal counsel. When the divorce agreement is signed and it is already too late, you will have to live with regret and deal with the financial fallout on your own. **FYI: You cannot appeal a bad deal.**

3. One side is stalling and time is being wasted with no progress.

Mediation is not marriage counseling, although it is a great process to improve communication, build up trust, and resolve family disputes. However, beware any mediation process where there is no progress being made for weeks and months at a time. In the wrong hands, mediation can be used as a stall tactic that costs you dearly in time and money. In a worst case scenario, a bad intentioned spouse can use the time spent during divorce mediation to hide assets or income, or inflate debts.

4. You need legal action.

This is one of the biggest limitations of mediation. Mediation is a voluntary process and it only works if both sides cooperate fully with financial disclosure. If your spouse refuses to cooperate, or is deceptive the mediator (or any out of court process) cannot remedy this. A mediator cannot subpoena documents get you a restraining order if assets are being dissipated or transferred, or give you legal advice to protect you.

AVOIDING MISTAKES:

When You Need Your Own Lawyer

Perhaps you are still on the fence about whether you need to retain your own lawyer, and which process will best protect your rights.   What "red flags" should you look for before you decide?

Red Flags for Communication / Custody:

Domestic Violence

Mental Illness, substance abuse and neglect issues

Parental alienation

Poor or nonexistent communication with your spouse

Spouse is a bully or controlling

Financial Red Flags:

Family Business or other Business Partnership

Hidden or Undisclosed Assets

Unreported Income

Complex asset valuation issues such as stock options, bonus and deferred compensation

Complex separate property issues (separate and marital property commingled)

Complex debts, including tax debts, mortgage foreclosure, bankruptcy

If one of the above scenarios exist in your case, **do yourself a big favor,** and schedule a consult with your own lawyer to ask about how the red flag might affect the outcome of your case.   Even if none of the above issues exist in your case, the number one reason to have your own counsel is having the benefit of expert advice to guide you every step of the way. (Yes, yes I know that I'm a lawyer, and obviously lawyers have a financial motivation to recommend that clients pay for legal advice, but still, divorce litigation is no place for an amateur.) Having your own advocate is the best way to ensure that costly mistakes are not made in your case, and that you understand all of the terms, obligations and consequences of your divorce agreement before you sign it[10]. There is a lot of language in a divorce contract that can significantly affect you and your children for the rest of your life. Having an attorney review the agreement and explain it to you is often the best move to ensure your financial security and most importantly, peace of mind.

No, Bob, we "charge legal fees".
We don't "plunder".

---

[10] Most divorce agreements are between 30 and 75 pages long! Make sure you fully understand your rights and responsibilities before you sign your agreement.

THE PSYCHOLOGY OF MONEY

Negotiating about money matters is one of the most challenging tasks there is. Money is the cornerstone of our financial security, with many issues taking root during childhood. Money decisions affect our past, our present, and of course our future. Money influences our hopes, dreams, fears, anxieties and our priorities. Simply put, money touches every part of our existence, our emotions, and our identity. It is no wonder then that financial negotiations during divorce are so complex and difficult to resolve.

5.

THE SMART SPLIT SOLUTION

5

SETTING THE STAGE FOR SUCCESS

Most clients and couples that I work with realize that a "War of the Roses" is most definitely **not** what they want.   They are seeking an affordable and reasonable divorce process, which I call the "Smart Split".   The Smart Split is a realistic and achievable solution for many couples, but it needs to be the goal for **both** parties, and it needs to be supported and encouraged by the parties' respective attorneys and advisors. Indeed, all couples, even those with six figure incomes, ample savings and retirement assets should be concerned about saving time, money and assets during a divorce. As stressed in the earlier chapters of this book, overcoming emotional obstacles, especially anger, is key to having a Smart Split. When given the option, "Unsubscribe" from feelings of anger and negativity.

CENTS AND SENSIBILITY

How can you set the stage for a Smart Split? It basically comes down to a commitment by both parties to reduce animosity, utilize what I call a "business deal mindset" and give their full efforts to negotiate a settlement. Both parties must be willing to communicate and

negotiate without hostility. This entails keeping an open mind to settlement possibilities, and

being willing to compromise[11]. Both parties should consider using an **out of court process**

(being mindful of the caveats set forth in the previous chapter). Secondly, parties should

devote their efforts to reaching a custody and parental access agreement which provides the

least disruption to the children. Options for joint custody and shared parenting time should be

explored. With most American households having two working parents, shared parenting is

often the most practical arrangement in the best interests of the children. Attorneys can help

their clients create a customized co-parenting schedule to meet the needs of the whole family.

As to financial issues, it is extremely important for parties to be realistic about their expectations, to be up front about their assets and income, and to produce necessary documentation in a timely and transparent manner. "Lifestyle" expenses such as nannies, vacations, private schools,

> *Divorce is the one human tragedy that reduces everything to cash.* -- Rita Mae Brown

extracurricular activities, private tutors and camps must be looked at carefully and with a view

towards compromise. It is important to realize that many issues related to the children,

including support and parenting time, are not "written in stone" forever. Issues relating to

children may in fact be modifiable later on in court after the divorce is settled, based upon a

---

[11] If your (or your spouse's) mindset is "my way or the highway", with one winner and one loser in the negotiation, a Smart Split is not likely to happen. In order to be successful, negotiations must take place in an atmosphere of "win win", where each party feels that their important goals are being addressed, and there are compromises made when necessary to reach a resolution.

demonstrated change of circumstances. An experienced attorney can guide you on issues which concern you, since the guidelines vary from state to state.

Regrettably, a Smart Split is simply not possible in every case because litigation cannot always be avoided. Some cases are more complex and will necessarily cost more to handle and take longer to reach the finish line. These cases often require the use of court ordered neutral experts or forensic appraisals. These include high conflict cases where there are issues of abuse, domestic violence, mental illness, drug and alcohol issues, paternity issues, hidden assets or income, a family business or professional practice, or separate property issues. It is also more challenging to resolve a case when one party has completely unrealistic demands, or a vindictive streak that gets in the way of negotiations.

I have lived a long life and had many troubles, most of which never happened.

--Mark Twain

MANAGING EXPECTATIONS

In those high conflict or complex asset divorce cases, I counsel my clients to be careful of their expectations, and to work together with me to adjust strategy on a periodic basis. I believe my clients are entitled to honest, straightforward advice about what is really going on in their case, and what the real obstacles are with regard to resolving issues. A "sugarcoated" picture helps no one, and leads to slippery logic, as well as distorted and thwarted expectations as to the costs, timeline, and obligations related to the divorce process. It is very common for clients to feel overwhelming disappointment and frustration by the high costs, delays and difficulties in a contested lawsuit. From an emotional and psychological standpoint, clients in protracted proceedings need to put the court proceedings in perspective, shifting their focus to other areas of their lives, including their outside interests, careers, and social relationships. It

> *Expectations say a huge amount about us and nothing about other people. This is because expectations are primarily unspoken, unstated demands. Disappointment is often a foregone conclusion.*
>
> -- Dr. Joy Browne

is not healthy to obsess or become bitter about a slow moving case – it only makes the process seem longer and even more frustrating to deal with. Realize that a contested case is a marathon, not a sprint, and adjust your expectations accordingly. Accept the fact that in some rare cases, the only way out is to wait for a ruling from the court. Don't throw in the towel and give up if doing so is against your financial and legal best interests[12]. Work together with your

lawyer to develop cost effective strategies in your case.   Bottom line: Even in an uphill battle,

in a winner-takes-all environment, you can survive and even thrive.

---

[12] Very often, the opposing party is stonewalling and offering you a flimsy deal in the hopes that you will give up. Discuss the pros and cons of the deal with your lawyer to assess whether it is still worth waiting for a final ruling from the court.

ASSESSING OPTIONS FOR SETTLEMENT

That moment comes in virtually every case, and not a moment too soon. The income and assets are identified. The expenses and liabilities are documented. The appraisals are completed, and you have reviewed them with your lawyer. All of the elements are in place, and it is an opportune time to structure a settlement agreement.

I make mistakes. I'll be the second to admit it.

-- Jean Kerr

At this stage, your lawyer should be actively working with opposing counsel to make a deal. Deals are made between lawyers by various methods: phone calls between the lawyers, conversations while they are in court handling other matters, emails, proposal letters, and face to face meetings. Your lawyer should be in touch with you on a regular basis regarding progress on the case.

If your lawyer isn't in touch with you regarding settlement possibilities, then contact his office and find out why. (**FYI:** It might be time to change your lawyer.) Sometimes, there are factors beyond your lawyer's control that are holding up the settlement process. Most often however, one side is stonewalling, or making unreasonable demands, which is creating an impasse in the negotiations. You need to figure out what the hold-up is, but how?

KEY QUESTIONS TO ASK YOUR LAWYER:

- *What are the terms you suggest for settlement?*

- *Are you satisfied that you have all of the information you need regarding the income, expenses, assets and debts pertaining to my case? If not, what information do you need, and how can you obtain it?*

- *Do I need to retain any experts at this stage?*

- *Are other appraisals needed?*

- *Are my requests reasonable?*

- *What is holding up the settlement?*

- *Can you schedule a four-way meeting with the other side so that we can discuss unresolved issues?*

- *Can written proposals be exchanged by correspondence or email?*

LET'S GET REAL

After several back and forth discussions with opposing counsel, at some point, your attorney may recommend to you that you review the terms of a proposed settlement agreement. He or she will explain that you are being offered your fair share of assets, along with a just outcome regarding custody and financial support.

Your attorney might even urge you to settle, warning you of negative consequences if you don't. But perhaps you are not ready to commit to the terms that are being proposed.

Instead, you think it might be a better strategy to drag the process out. You think that your spouse might give in to your demands if you hold out long enough. After all, no one can force you to accept terms that you are not happy with. If this is the mindset you hold, and your lawyer is still urging you to sign the agreement, then **recognize that maybe you are the problem.** Perhaps it's time for you to step outside your comfort zone and face up to your role in this conflict.

QUESTIONS TO ASK YOURSELF (BE HONEST!):

- *What is holding me back from accepting the terms?*

- *Are the terms I am demanding fair and reasonable?*

- *Are there areas where I can compromise?*

- *What can I do to make this settlement happen?*

- *Are the legal fees worth it?*

- *What are the risks if I refuse to settle?*

- *What is the worst case scenario?*

- *What is my motivation here?*

You should realize that there is a real price to be paid for extending a divorce case and refusing to settle. And in case you need to hear it again, **that price is paid in time, money and aggravation.** A protracted lawsuit means days missed from work, tense days spent in court or in your lawyer's office, and less money to go around for other necessities. Certainly, there is nothing wrong with taking an aggressive, bottom line approach to a financial negotiation. In fact, with a 'take it or leave it' strategy, you might prevail in getting some ginormous concessions from your ex. However, if you decide to play hardball, be aware of the risks, and make sure you are willing to pay the price[13]. Don't pin your hopes on the remote chance that your ex will pay your legal fees. In many cases, there is zero chance of this happening. Don't live in denial.

When all is said and done, if the final outcome doesn't go your way, take responsibility. **Don't blame your lawyer, the other lawyer, the "system" or the Judge for your disappointment, or the sky high legal costs. Own it, and move forward.**

Developing a Game Plan
for the Marital Residence

During a separation or divorce, making a decision regarding the marital residence *(Who stays? Who goes? Sell to a third party or buy out your spouse?)* is one that has to be made sooner or later. Until the parties reach a full agreement on the issue, or the judge orders the sale of the residence, divorcing couples are usually forced to endure living together as reluctant roommates. It is not uncommon for both parties to dig in their heels, both insisting on keeping the house and refusing to compromise.

> *Well, after the divorce, I went home and turned all the lights on!* --Larry David

---

[13] That price could very well include an award of counsel fees to your ex. If the Court determines that your position in the case is unreasonable, and that you (and your lawyer) are driving up legal fees in the case, watch out! If you have a problem paying your own legal fees, take my word for it: You will hate paying your ex spouse's legal fees even more.

The stonewalling can last for months or years until one side gives in, or a full settlement is reached with concessions made on both sides.

In one recent case, my client was a firefighter with joint custody rights who moved into the basement of the marital residence. His wife and children lived upstairs. Neither party could afford to buy out the other, and they both agreed that it was not the right time to sell the house. The parties agreed to share the house expenses proportionately, in accordance with their income. Moreover, the children were able to stay in their home, and see both parents on a daily basis, which was in their best interests. The parties managed to successfully maintain the upstairs / downstairs arrangement for nearly two years, until the house was finally sold in a favorable real estate market. This scenario[14] was clearly a **win-win** for both parties.

In another case I handled recently, a mature couple in their sixties were living together while they went through years of divorce proceedings. Their bickering and fighting over the household bills led to "the remote control incident". During one of their many arguments, the wife threw the remote control at her husband. He threw it back at her. They were both subsequently arrested, and became involved in protracted family offense proceedings and criminal court proceedings. Needless to say, they both learned a harsh and expensive lesson. My client, the husband, finally agreed to move out of the house. Shortly thereafter, the parties cooperated in the sale of their house. By that time, the mortgage had

---

[14] This custody arrangement is a version of "nesting" and it is an increasingly popular trend in custody matters. If parents can separate informally (i.e. not legal separated) while living in the same house, they can create customized parenting plans that cause the least disruption to the children. Many separated and divorced couples continue to share holidays, birthdays, and even vacations together as part of the nesting arrangement.

gone unpaid for nearly six months, and there was virtually no equity left. This scenario was a

lose-lose all around.

THERE ARE ONLY A FEW BASIC OPTIONS WHEN IT COMES TO THE MARITAL RESIDENCE

OPTION ONE: The house is sold on the open market to a third party for fair market value, and the net proceeds are divided, usually 50/50.

OPTION TWO: The parties agree that one party will move out, and the other party stays in the house with the children for an agreed upon time period, such as the youngest child's graduation from high school.

OPTION THREE: One side buys out the other's share of equity, after a neutral appraisal to determine fair market value. The buyout can be in the form of cash, or an offset against other marital assets. You can also obtain financing for the buyout, including mortgage refinancing, a second mortgage, an equity line of credit, a home equity loan (HELOC), borrowing from retirement assets, or a loan from family.

OPTION FOUR: One or both parties remain in the house until there is a foreclosure or short sale.

Like it or not, in a cash crunched economy, especially in pricey or stagnant housing markets, being reluctant roommates with your ex is a trend that is here to stay. Discuss each of the above options with your attorney, and explore whether a consensus can be reached on which route to take. Here are some legal and financial pointers to make the transition from spouse to roommate a bit smoother, while you are still living under one roof:

1. **Decide together how to share time with the children.** If parents continue living in the house together during a divorce, it is very critical that certain ground rules be in place concerning sharing time with the children, getting them to school or their sports practices, and paying for their expenses, including child care, activities, and medical expenses. Whenever possible, the parties should agree to maintain the status quo that existed prior to the breakup. When it comes to discipline, parents must present a united front and a uniform parenting style. Lax parenting rules (especially during a divorce) often breed trouble, especially with teenagers.

2. **Make a fair agreement on how to share the household bills**, including payment of the mortgage, taxes, insurance, landscaping and utilities. These expenses are typically apportioned based on each party's income[15]. It is also important to discuss who is going to pay for needed repairs, especially if the marital residence is going to be sold.

3. **Consult with professionals to make joint decisions** regarding a refinance of the mortgage to get a better interest rate, or a loan modification. Cooperation and good faith between divorcing couples are essential if the house is going to be listed for sale and shown to prospective buyers. If selling your house quickly and at the best price is a priority, then go to the top listing real estate broker in your area. Do not use your cousin or friend from the PTA, or someone who

---

[15] An example of a *pro rata* apportionment is as follows: If Wife earns $100,000 per year and Husband earns $50,000, then the parties' respective obligations would be 66% and 34%.

charges a lower commission. In the long run, you will pay heavily in time and money if you don't use the best professional available.

4.   **Make every effort to "take the high road".** Therapy can be very helpful to purge or at least manage your anger, and this creates a much healthier atmosphere for both parents and the children in the house. Focus on making compromises, reaching a fair deal and sticking to it. Of course, this is easier said than done, but self-restraint and dealing with your ex in a business-like manner can go a long way.

5.   **Tax Consequences**: Don't forget to get advice from your lawyer or accountant regarding tax consequences related to the residence, including which party gets the right to the deductions such as mortgage interest and property taxes, and how to apportion any capital gains or other taxes due upon the sale.

6.   **Personal Property**: The furnishings and property in the marital residence need to be shared in an equitable manner. Make a list, and flip a coin if needed to agree on how the stuff gets divided. Don't pay your lawyer hundreds of dollars per hour to negotiate how to divide up used furniture or the junk piled up in the garage. Just don't.

POP QUIZ #1

Circle 5 words and phrases that resonate with you:

Co-parenting	*Going for the Jugular*
Family Therapy	*Joint custody*
"I'm not giving up a dime"	*Resolving issues*
Day in Court	*Betrayal*
Not my fault	*Change*
Ready to move on	*Settlement*
Revenge	*"You owe me"*
Forgiveness	*Compromise*
Aggressive lawyer	*Going to Trial*
Communication	*Closure*
Never, no way	*"I'll pay my lawyer before I pay my spouse"*
Fear about the future	*I deserve more*
"Poor me"	*"Let the Judge put me in jail!"*

What do the circled words say about where you are at this point in the process?

F.O.R.G.I.V.E.N.E.S.S. and LETTING GO

Adopting the game-changing mindset of forgiveness is the key to resolving many protracted disputes, including divorce conflicts. Based on my experience with my clients, an apology can heal wounds and mend rifts even better than a pile of money! Sadly, accepting personal responsibility is often seen as a weakness, not a moral virtue. Here are some other thoughts in this same vein, which I hope will persuade you to forgive (if not forget):

- Forgiveness is not always easy. At times, it feels more painful than the wound we suffered, to forgive the one who inflicted it. And yet, there is no peace without forgiveness. (Marianne Williamson)

- Forgiveness means giving up all hope for a better past. (Lily Tomlin)

- Holding on to anger is like taking poison and waiting for your enemy to die. (Unknown)

- It's one of the greatest gifts you can give yourself, to forgive. Forgive everybody. (Maya Angelou)

- The weak can never forgive. Forgiveness is the attribute of the strong. (Mahatma Gandhi)

- It's okay to be sad. Own it! Here is a simple exercise to work through it. Take in a deep inhale and feel what is coming into your lungs. Say to yourself, "This is life. This is real." Be in that moment and if emotion wells up, let it come! Allow this truth to flow and understand that love is never lost. It just gets redirected. This is the state of affairs today, but it is not your entire life. (Donna Martini)

- Always forgive your enemies. Nothing annoys them so much. (Oscar Wilde)

- Darkness cannot drive out darkness; only light can do that. Hate cannot drive out hate; only love can do that. (Martin Luther King Jr.)

- Apologies have enormous value, independent of any monetary settlement…One of the dirty little secrets of the legal system is that if people could simply learn how to apologize, lawyers and judges would be out of work. (Thane Rosenbaum)

IF YOU CAN FORGIVE, YOU CAN CHANGE YOUR FUTURE.

RECREATE YOURSELF

By Eileen Ansel Wolpe[16]

Divorce is a hard path, a long, circuitous journey that is not something you can control. You open the door and walk through it, thinking you will go to destination 'x' only to find out that it was just an illusion, that destination 'x' is only visible from inside the marriage and that once you leave, you not only cannot find it, but you start to realize, it probably never existed at all.... What I'm trying to say is that everything changes. In ways you can't imagine or anticipate. Everything. Everything. Everything.

If you can stomach the loneliness (extreme and painful at times), then you have a chance. Only then do you have a real chance to grow, to change, to learn who you are, why you ended up where you did, how you came to be there, where you want to go. All of it. The best of it. The worst of it. And everything in between. You begin to think in a new way, free of the paradigms and mind prisons that had to be created in order to keep a broken marriage functioning. You learn to see with different parts of your brain, of your life, even parts you (arrogantly) thought you were already using. You find them anew and realize they're dusty and old and in need of polishing and repair. You tucked them away long ago, you had to, there was no room for them in that relationship. On and on it goes. Divorce is a tearing apart of togetherness. It is a rendering of all things built to keep you comfortable and safe. It is the destruction of together-dreams, forever-dreams, family-dreams, love-dreams. You cannot leave a marriage without doing violence to all those things, no matter how amicable the divorce.

Even the word 'divorce.' It's a cleaver. A great big bloody butcher knife that slices through even the most connected hearts. There is no way around that. It's why all the

---

[16] previously married to, and amicably divorced from, Rabbi David Wolpe.

mythology of divorce is what it is. Because there is truth in those myths. When you walk out the door, which may well be the bravest moment of your life, you are suddenly at sea, not on a path. The earth ceases to be solid beneath your feet and you are drowning in quicksand. You thought you would fly but you sink and the only way you will survive is if you intuit that you must be still until the universe begins to solidify around you once again. Only then can you begin to move. I care too much not to warn you. You cannot see what lies beyond the frame around the door that is the exit. It is not possible. It is a death. And just like life's death, you are not permitted to see beyond the threshold. But I have been here for the past year and I can tell you it looks nothing like it does from inside the threshold. It is a foreign, inhospitable, dangerous journey. One that holds infinite, endless gifts for the ones who are brave enough to continue on, and will eat alive those who misstep, or throw them instantly back in through a different door with a different partner.

The goal of divorce should not be to be with someone else. There is no one else. Not yet. Because in order for there to be anyone else, first you have to recreate yourself. And that, as you know, is a task only for the very bravest of heart. It takes stamina, fortitude, faith, trust, belief and not a small measure of complete insanity. It takes time. To forge a new suit of armor. Made from better material. Something new. Something more flexible. Breathable. Fire resistant. Softer. Easier. More comfortable. It takes time to regrow bones and skin and sinew and soul. It takes courage not to thrash about in the quicksand. It takes a willingness to surrender completely to every weakness inside yourself, to forgive, forgive, forgive... and to let go. Only then do you really have a chance. Only then can you begin to walk towards a new place, a better place. Only then will you know that you have done the right thing.

6.

REALITY CHECK

6

YOUR LOVE / HATE RELATIONSHIP WITH YOUR LAWYER

So far, this book has covered many of the legal issues that individuals will encounter in their separation or divorce process. As you have seen, I encourage my clients to choose a simpler, saner approach to their case, to take the high road whenever possible, and to avoid unnecessary litigation. However, this book cannot possibly cover every divorce scenario or strategy, and is not intended to be a substitute to getting legal advice. You should definitely consult with

In Palm Springs, they think homelessness is caused by bad divorce lawyers. -- Garry Trudeau

your own attorney to learn how to best protect your legal and financial rights in your divorce.

Since the time of Shakespeare[17] and likely well before that, it has been popular in our culture to disparage attorneys. It goes without saying that there are good and bad divorce attorneys, just like there are good and bad apples in any bunch. As a consumer of professional services, it is incumbent on **you** to do your research and to find a divorce attorney who is qualified and caring, as well as affordable. The top two criteria in choosing an attorney are:

---

[17] "The first thing we do, let's kill all the lawyers." William Shakespeare's *Henry VI, Part 2.*

- *The attorney is experienced in divorce and family law.*

- *The attorney practices law in your county or jurisdiction.*

Once you have narrowed down your search based on the top two criteria listed above, it is up to you to find the lawyer that best suits you and your case. I strongly recommend that you personally *interview at least three* attorneys before you make a decision to hire one. Be wary of any attorney who claims guaranteed results.

> *I don't want a lawyer to tell me what I cannot do; I hire him to tell me how to do what I want to do.*
> -- J.P. Morgan

Make sure you feel comfortable with your lawyer and his or her staff, and do not feel intimidated by them. Your relationship with your lawyer must be one of trust, because you will be sharing very intimate details about your life, your children, and your finances. Since it is a relationship that will affect the rest of your life, make sure that the attorney that you choose is a good fit for you and your case.

Most divorce attorneys are ethical, hardworking and client focused. However, one of the chief complaints clients have about their attorneys is that they don't get a call or email back from them. There is simply no excuse for this! If your lawyer or his/her staff does not respond to you in a timely manner (by the end of the business day) then consider changing your lawyer. After all, if your lawyer is not calling you back, very likely he is not calling back the opposing attorney, or the Judge's staff. If your case is not attended to by your lawyer, then it will take longer to get resolved. Even more importantly, many issues in divorce cases have a tendency of escalating overnight if the lawyers

> *He who said "Talk is Cheap" has never hired a lawyer.*
> --Anonymous

are not responsive to their clients or opposing counsel. **Bottom line:** You are paying a lot of money to a professional to help you with your case, and you deserve a responsive and dedicated attorney working on your case.

Be very wary if your lawyer is openly contemptuous of your spouse's lawyer or the judge assigned to your case. You want your lawyer to be a strong advocate for you, but you need him/her to get along with the other professionals in your case. If there is excessive friction, or a personal animosity between the lawyers, this will cost you.

YOUR SKIN IN THE GAME

In addition, be very mindful about your legal fees. Review your bills, and don't hesitate to question billing charges that you don't understand or agree with. Be assertive. In most cases, you will be responsible to pay all or most of your own legal fees, so don't run a large tab and then get angry at your lawyer when the balances climb every month. The day of reckoning will come. In many cases, who pays for the legal fees (and how) becomes one of the last financial issues to be resolved in the divorce. Don't let your legal fees become part of the problem. Discuss the issue of fees openly with your lawyer, and be vigilant about the costs and strategies employed in your case.

> *The trouble with the legal profession is that 98% of its members give the rest a bad name.*
>
> -- Anonymous

UNDERSTAND
YOUR LAWYER'S ROLE

You have selected an experienced matrimonial lawyer to represent you in your case,

and you have high expectations of his or her abilities, (as

you should!) But the first thing you must realize and accept

is that your lawyer is not a miracle worker who can solve

your problems overnight.   Even at $600 per hour, your

lawyer is not a magician who can make your problems (or

I'm trusting in the Lord and a good lawyer.
-- Oliver North

your spouse) disappear. The messier your finances (and emotions) are, the longer it will take

to sort it out and to find ways to resolve legal claims. If you and your spouse have been

fighting over a recent infidelity, or have taken years to decide that it is time to end your

dysfunctional relationship, then it will take a while to reduce or eliminate the emotional

factors that get in the way of resolving your case. There are very few easy and quick solutions

in matrimonial matters.   Virtually every decision you make will have fallout, both good and

bad. **You must keep your expectations in check, and that includes expectations of what your**

lawyer can reasonably accomplish in your case in a few weeks or months.

Clients inevitably ask two questions at the beginning of their case: *"How long will it take*

to get divorced?" and of course ,*"How much will this*

In law, nothing is certain but the expense.
-- Samuel Butler

cost?" Hear ye. Hear ye. Unless your case is a Simple

Uncontested or Mediation matter, the honest answer to

those two questions is, in legal parlance: *"It depends."* No lawyer can give you a definite answer to these crucial questions, because there are no definite answers. If there are multiple issues to be analyzed in your case, the time frame and cost of the case will depend on many factors beyond your lawyer's control. Most significantly, these factors are (*drum roll, please*):

FACTORS BEYOND YOUR LAWYER'S CONTROL

- **the law applicable to your case;**

- **the facts of your case;**

- **the judge assigned;**

- **the other lawyer's modus operandi or strategy;**

- **your spouse's willingness to agree on reasonable terms.**

There are very few guaranteed outcomes in divorce cases. As stated earlier, family law, with all of its emotional overtones, fact specific determinations, and legal 'gray areas', is far from an exact science. Your lawyer's opinion about results that can be achieved is generally based upon *ranges of probability* which, in turn, are based upon the facts which you provide, and the law in your jurisdiction. Even if you have a phalanx of the best, highest paid lawyers on your side, sometimes it just comes down to: **The law is the law and the facts are the facts. In other words, it is what it is.**

UNREALISTIC EXPECTATIONS

Clients expect their lawyers to take over and take all of the necessary steps to ensure the best possible outcome. They expect the lawyer to correctly evaluate their case, to tell them when to show up in Court, and where to collect the settlement check. For the cost of their retainer, they want their lawyer to completely annihilate the other side.   And they imagine a quick result, just like they see in the movies, or on television. Their lawyer will file a lawsuit, prove the claim by making a slam dunk legal argument, and then bring the other side to their knees and settle.

Reality, especially in divorce cases, rarely works out that way.

In real life legal disputes, it is rare to find one side that is 100% right, and the other side is 100% wrong. A lawsuit almost always is met with a countersuit.   Your friends may egg you on, saying, "Go sue that SOB and take him for every penny." It often feels good and sounds good to hear that kind of support. But it can also get you into big trouble.

Observing my children growing up, I have seen my share of disputes over toys, space in the bathroom, and use of the car. When one child wrongfully takes the property of the other, the aggrieved child is hurt and angry at having their property snatched and their space violated. The first reaction is to scream, yell and most of all, get even. As a litigator, I am very familiar with this kind of reaction. I see this vindictive impulse nearly every time a broken hearted client stomps into my office. They are seething, and they want satisfaction.   In most cases, their emotions have overtaken their reason, and they want to win at all costs. Later on, they might have buyer's remorse. Their legal strategy had led them to wipe out their vacation money and life savings. Or worse, put them on the path to foreclosure or bankruptcy.

Protracted lawsuits are usually the result of emotion. Always remember, lawyers are in the lawsuit business. If you are angry and you want to sue, a lawyer can accommodate you easily. If your mindset is, "I'm furious, and I want my spouse to pay", take a moment to think it through. Take a Time Out and ask yourself: What am I getting into? Is this lawsuit a good investment of my time, money and emotion? Make a "business" decision and look for a "business" solution.   Analyze the pros and cons. Obtain advice from an experienced professional and find out: How strong is your claim, and what damages can you recover? How much time and money must you commit to pursuing your claim? Keep in mind that going through a bitter, protracted litigation can harm you more than the original trauma of your break up.   A lawsuit is usually a two to three year ordeal, with delays, pressures, risks and exorbitant costs. It can be unpredictable and extremely frustrating. Look before you leap. Consider turning the other cheek. You might just come out ahead.

What <u>should</u> you reasonably expect from your lawyer?

1.   Provides you with an analysis of the facts of your case, the legal issues involved, and an assessment of your legal rights and obligations;

2.   Delivers expert representation and negotiation on your behalf with regard to all issues;

3.   Informs you and advises you about the law in your jurisdiction, the legal procedures and process, as well as reasonable settlement possibilities;

4.   Advises you about the risks in the process, including costs, or court rulings that might go against you;

5.   Refers you to other experts that might be helpful in your case (Refer to Step 5 of the Master List);

6.   Makes reasonable predictions of how the court might rule in your case if there is a trial, and whether a settlement before trial is in your best interest.

     FYI: A settlement before trial is nearly always in your best interest.

7.   Responds to your calls and emails expeditiously and is willing to meet with you in the office to address your concerns;

8.   Reassures you and is empathetic regarding the emotional toll of the case. Your lawyer is not just a professional giving you advice. Your lawyer is a *counselor at law.* A good lawyer will keep you steady, and ensure that you are not going through this process alone.

PENNY WISE, POUND FOOLISH?

The viability of many legal claims in a divorce case is based upon what you can prove via documents or other credible evidence. Don't blame your lawyer if you cannot back up your claims with documentation. For example, if

He is no lawyer who cannot take two sides.
-- Charles Lamb

you claim that your parents gave you $25,000 as a gift when you bought the marital residence fifteen years ago, and you want that money to be credited back to you in the divorce settlement, you must furnish proof of the $25,000 gift. Don't expect the court or the opposing attorney to take your word for it. Listen closely when when your lawyer gives you advice about strategy and settlement. Inquire whether pursuing certain financial claims is worth the cost. Does it make sense to spend $10,000 in attorney fees to do multi-day depositions, or

Compromise is the best and cheapest lawyer.
-- Robert Louis Stevenson

serve two dozen subpoenas, when the financial issue at stake is only $25,000 and the ultimate outcome is unclear? If you have to guess, the answer is probably "No". You must ask yourself whether the time, stress, and cost of a full blown legal battle are worth it in the end. Don't make mountains out of molehills, and then expect someone else to foot the bill. If you run up a big legal bill, you must take responsibility for it and move on. **Bottom Line**: Your lawyer's job is to put in the time to investigate and pursue the claim and thereby earn his or her fee. Always remember that you are being billed for your lawyer's time and expertise, not the final outcome.

CUSTODY PITFALLS TO AVOID

How to Lose Legal Custody
of Your Child in 7 Easy Steps

From the outset, it is important for mothers and fathers to recognize that married parents start out with *joint custody* rights of their minor children. This means that both parents have *equal* rights to their children, and the same right to pursue custody of their children in their divorce case. In a world where most households contain two working parents, and many fathers have an active role in raising their children, the presumption that mothers will automatically get custody no longer exists. In fact, statistics show that fathers who seek custody of their children, are awarded custody 50% of the time. Custody laws in most states are gender neutral, and this means that when the facts of a given case are applied to the governing law, a court may determine that it is in the best interests of the child to live primarily with the father, or the mother, or 50/50 with both parents. If you are a parent and you want to prevail in your custody goals, steer clear of the following:

1. Not being the primary caretaker:

In most households, one parent is most responsible for caring for the children's basic needs -- the so called primary caretaker. The parent who is the most involved in the children's daily lives usually has the edge in a custody case. Therefore, if you are not putting in the time to do homework with your child, feeding, bathing, reading, taking him or her to the bus stop, you are at a disadvantage in a custody case. There is no better way to lose custody than to demonstrate to a judge that you are simply not involved in raising your child.

2. Not being active in your child's schedule and activities:

Do you know the names of your child's teachers? Have you ever supervised your child on a play date or taken your child to the doctor? Do you regularly attend school conferences and school events? If the answer to these is "no", then it is an indication that someone else (i.e. the other parent) is the primary caretaker, not you.

3. Alcohol, drugs, or other "parental fitness" issues:

A parent who even casually partakes in alcohol and/or drugs will have a problem in winning custody. Most judges will take allegations of substance abuse seriously, and these allegations will be investigated thoroughly via random testing, psychological evaluations, and interviews. If you have an issue with substance abuse, then seek treatment for it immediately. If you are the perpetrator of domestic violence or abuse (which often goes hand in hand with alcohol use), this also pretty much guarantees that you will lose custody.

4. Leaving a paper trail that will hang you in Court:

Thanks to new technology, virtually every custody trial features the submission of evidence that can be used to portray the other parent in a very damaging light. Sometimes the evidence can make or break the custody case. The evidence can include text messages, photos and negative emails. Also potentially harmful are video and voice mail recordings (a la Alec

Baldwin).   If you are prone to sending impulsive emails and texts, ranting and raving at the other parent, third parties, or your own child, you are at risk of losing custody.

5. Disparaging the other parent.

Judges tend to look favorably upon a parent who demonstrates that he/she supports the child's relationship with the other parent. A parent who is constantly denigrating the other parent, "leaking" anger, and negatively influencing the child's relationship with the noncustodial parent will be reprimanded. In extreme cases, there will be allegations of parental alienation and interference with parenting time. Many judges will consider a change of custody if this type of interference is shown. Bottom line: if you want to show the Judge that you will promote the best interests of your child,

> *If you practice maintaining your composure, and remember that someone else's behavior belongs to that person and cannot upset you unless you allow it to do so, then you will not become an unwilling target.*
>
> -- Wayne Dyer

then you need to show that you recognize the value of the child's relationship with your ex, and will take the steps to encourage that relationship. Of course, when you are going through an adversarial proceeding with someone you don't like very much, it can be very hard to put those feelings aside for the sake of your child. But that is exactly what you need to do if you want to prevail in your case.

6. Showing lack of control:

It is critical to consistently act with good judgment and self control if you want to prevail in a custody case. A parent who regularly loses control, and who cannot control his/her anger will be at a disadvantage. I have handled many cases where a litigant will behave appallingly

right in the courtroom, in front of the Judge. An angry outburst in court will be remembered.

Similarly, a parent who "acts out" in front of the child's attorney, social workers, teachers,

neighbors, etc. will find himself confronted with a lot of negative testimony and evidence at

trial. This is where the voice mails and emails also come into play. If you are serious about

winning custody, then you must exhibit self-control and put your child's needs first. Going

through a divorce is a difficult, emotional process. A custody case raises the stakes

considerably. If necessary, seek counseling to get your anger under control. At the very

least, taking this step will likely lead to improved relationships with your ex, other third parties,

family members, and your child.

7. Failing to follow your attorney's advice:

Going through a divorce and/or custody proceeding is one of the most stressful

experiences there is. Whether you are seeking primary custody of your children, joint decision

making, or a customized parenting plan, your goal should be to survive the process while

protecting your rights to your most valuable asset -- your children. It is critical that you seek

out the advice of an experienced family law attorney, who has handled contested custody trials

(not the attorney who did the closing on your house, or the lawyer who charges the lowest

retainer to do an uncontested divorce.) With an experienced advocate by your side, you can

avoid making the mistakes outlined above, and you will greatly improve the odds of success in

your custody case.

TAKE AWAY CUSTODY STRATEGIES

- It is important to be aware that once a child reaches a certain age (11 or older in most jurisdictions) the child gets a strong vote regarding custody and the parenting schedule. Teenagers pretty much get to live with who they want, and spend time with the other parent based on the schedule they want. (FYI: Thirteen is the new eighteen.)

- If you are in a contested custody case, assume you are being carefully monitored by the other parent. In today's world of smart phones and "instant evidence", a lawyer can make or break a custody case based upon lapses in judgment by one of the parents. Social media and other digital footprints are part of virtually every case. Instant evidence can include comments on blogs, Facebook posts, Snapchats, Instagram photos, emails, texts, photos and videos. Not only should you be cautious using social media, but you should instruct your friends and family to also be careful what they post online.

- Be civil and cooperative with your child's teachers, doctors, therapists and coaches. Not only is this common sense parenting advice, but in a custody case, these are potential witnesses who can be subpoenaed to testify against you. No matter what you do, don't burn bridges with potential witnesses.

- If your case is in court, there are a number of court appointed neutral professionals that will have a say in the outcome of your custody case. Be on your best behavior with the child's attorney, forensic custody evaluator, CPS social worker and parenting coordinator. Be courteous and well behaved in the presence of court personnel, and remember, everything that goes on in the courtroom and in the hallways outside the courtroom can and will be reported back to the Judge presiding over your case. Dress appropriately when you go to court. Be on time for every court appearance. In most cases, you will not get a second chance to make a good first impression with the Judge, so don't blow it.

Watch your thoughts; they become words.

Watch your words; they become actions.

Watch your actions, they become habits.

Watch your habits, they become character.

Watch your character; it becomes your destiny.

Frank Outlaw

REALITY-CHECK POP QUIZ #2

QUESTION #1:   **Which phrase best describes your current mindset?**

A: I am ready to move on with my life.

B: I am very uncertain about my future.

C: None of this is my fault.

QUESTION #2   **Which of the following do you believe?**

A: I am ready to make compromises to end this dispute.

B: I need more time / advice before I can commit to a settlement.

C: I want my "Day in Court" and I expect my spouse to pay the costs of this case, and to pay for what he / she has done to me.

QUESTION #3   **How would you describe your ex?**

A: He / she was not the best spouse, but he/she is a good co-parent.

B: I can't think of anything good to say.

C: My ex is a deadbeat, and my children are better off not knowing him/her.

QUESTION #4   **How would you complete this phrase?** Divorce is _____.

A: A new start.

B: Something I am very worried about and I hope to recover from.

C: Devastating. My life is over, and I will never be ok again.

Give yourself 2 points for each "A" answer, 1 point for each "B" answer, and 0 points for each "C" answer.

If you scored 7 or 8: Congratulations! You are in a good place, and moving forward with your life.

If you scored 3-6: You have a long road ahead, but a Smart Split is possible for you. Work closely with your lawyer and other professionals in your case. Focus on forward movement, realistic expectations and meaningful progress in reaching your goals.

If you scored 0-2: Your expectations are not in line with reality. It is time to look in the mirror and reassess your goals and expectations.

"Let's play house. I'll be the mommy and twice a month you can be daddy."

TOP 5 FINANCIAL RISKS FOR MARRIED WOMEN

Time for some tough love for readers of the fairer sex. Let's start with the good news. Women today have unprecedented power. They are better educated than men, and their earning power is ever increasing. Whether a woman is single, married, divorced, or widowed, chances are she is going to outlive her partner.[18] Now the not-so-good news. A married woman will be more adversely affected than a man by life's biggest landmines, including death of a spouse, and divorce. A woman's longevity is both an advantage and a huge challenge, because she will need more in savings to cover her basic expenses for an extended period of years, including medical expenses that escalate later in life. Women who stay home to care for their children, and who forego their careers are especially vulnerable when they are jettisoned aside by their once loving spouses. "Stay at home wife" is <u>not</u> a tenured position. Often too late, women face a financial reckoning

> *No one anticipates divorce when they are exchanging vows, and it can be devastating, emotionally and financially. To ease the financial side of the blow, you need to maintain your financial identity in your relationship. That means having your own credit history, your own credit card, and your own savings and retirement accounts.* — Jean Chatsky

---

[18] According to the U.S. Census Bureau, the current life expectancy for women is 80.5 years, compared to 75.5 years for men.

as they are sinking in quicksand. That is when they realize: *"A. Man. Is. Not. A. Financial. Plan"*.

What are the other risks that women face?

RISK # 1: Being Reactive, Not Proactive:

When I speak to married women, I am often alarmed by how in the dark they are about the economic nuts and bolts of their household and financial investments. It is so important to be proactive, not reactive about finances, whether you are single or married. No matter how trustworthy your spouse is, it is very risky to abdicate all financial decision making to another person. This includes tax planning, dealing with debts, and putting money into

Trust your husband, adore your husband, and get as much as you can in your own name. --Joan Rivers

savings. If you have no idea what is going in these areas, you have no one to blame but yourself if your credit is shot and your finances are in free fall. Find out where your money is and how it's doing. Be careful about paying expenses for adult children when you don't have savings or money set aside for retirement. The same goes for paying for private colleges when other more affordable options are available. You can take out a loan for college (which your children can repay) but there are no loans for retirement. Meet with a financial advisor without delay.

RISK #2:   Living with Blinders On:

Don't sign off on loan documents, or worse, sign and e-file tax returns without reading them. If there are financial secrets going on in your marriage, what I call 'financial infidelity', or bad money management, you need to find out. If all of your assets, including your residence and bank accounts, are in the name of your husband's family members, but the credit card debt is in your name, find out why. In a recent case that I handled, the husband urged the wife to sign a $250,000 home equity line of credit

> *Women enjoyed rights in Egypt they would not enjoy again for more than 2000 years. They owned ships, ran vineyards, filed lawsuits, and practiced medicine... Their power was unprecedented.*   --Stacy Schiff

(HELOC) three years before the marriage ended. At the time she signed the loan documents, she didn't care where the money went, because the marriage was stable, and the money was flowing[19]. By the time the divorce started, the husband had a girlfriend. Of course, my client was hell bent on proving that her husband spent the HELOC money on the girlfriend. Over $50,000 in legal fees was spent to try to trace the money and track down every expense, and it turned out most of it went to pay for home improvements and joint credit card balances with 30% interest. If my client had paid attention to the finances during the marriage, both parties would have saved a ton of money and aggravation in their divorce.

---

[19] As my mother likes to say, 'money is honey'.

RISK #3*:* Unreported income on Tax Returns:

This is a biggie. If you are enjoying the lifestyle brought about by cash or unreported income, then be super careful about your legal strategy, especially with regard to going in front of a Judge, and signing sworn affidavits regarding your income and assets. What you certify to the IRS on your joint tax returns might come back to bite you in a divorce. Many Judges will have no qualms about reporting you to the IRS if they see evidence of unreported taxable income. Even if you don't end up with an IRS issue, you can't waltz into divorce court and say, *Yes Judge, I knew my husband had cash income in his construction business, and during the good years, we both enjoyed spending that money, but now we are divorcing, and I don't agree with the income reported on our tax return, because now I expect him to support me based upon our previous lifestyle.*

RISK#4:
Not Getting Involved with Financial Planning:

Another reason why women need to take an active role with their finances is that women can actually do a better job than their spouse when it comes to investing. According to many studies, women's investment portfolios on average outperform men's, because men tend to trade stocks more frequently, which generates fees, and also tend to hold more volatile portfolios. (On the other hand, because women tend to be more risk-averse, they sometimes sacrifice growth opportunities for safety.)   My advice to you? Pay attention, and get involved in your investments and savings. Be a financial decision maker in your marriage.

RISK #5: Emotional + Living in Denial:

Generally speaking, women experience more stress, anxiety and emotional turmoil when a relationship turns bad. Maybe this is why statistics show that 80% of divorces are initiated by women. I counsel my women clients to focus on a 'bottom line' approach to negotiations, so that emotions don't get in the way of getting the best deal. Women also tend to trust their spouses and live in denial about legal and financial problems, such as debts, money judgments or risky

> *Most women outlive their spouses. Divorce remains at record rates. It's important for a woman to be able to control her finances.*
>
> -- Maria Bartiromo

investments. Ignoring these problems during marriage really hurts women. By the time the divorce comes around, the debt problem has escalated into a full scale legal disaster, to include bankruptcy and/or foreclosure. Even if you and your husband are completely broke with no assets, you may still be liable for IRS debts and other debts in a divorce.

Let's end this topic with more good news for everyone: It is never too late to make better financial decisions.

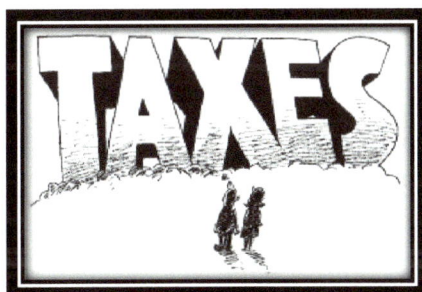

10 LITTLE KNOWN TRUTHS ABOUT GOING TO COURT

✓ Our culture and the adversarial legal system in the United States is a parallel universe, geared toward the idea that **divorce is a fight where one side wins and the other side loses**. Contested litigation is a bruising process, whether you win or not. High stakes divorce negotiations take place in a world which often defies neat categories and hard and fast rules. Always remembers that so called "shark" trial lawyers are highly paid gladiators, whose goal is to win the battle, not necessarily solve the problem. (**Caveat emptor**: the shark will eventually go after his own client to get paid the legal fees he is owed).

✓ **Your lawyer cannot control** your spouse, your spouse's lawyer, or how the other lawyer handles the case. Even if you try your hardest to keep legal costs down, the costs can escalate if the other side does not cooperate, delays the legal process, or insists on going to trial. Even if both sides cooperate with each other, some Judges have harrowing rules and requirements when it comes to the discovery process, motion practice, or pretrial submissions. This is not your lawyer's fault. Also, there might not be anything the Judge can do about stalling and the related costs, unless the delays are egregious, and the behavior of the other side obstructionist and/or frivolous.

✓ Despite what you may expect, **the Judge is not there to protect you**, or to punish your spouse. His or her job is to apply the law of your state to the facts of your case. In the "no fault" divorce era, most Judges do not care about your spouse's rampant adultery, or the fact that he sat on the couch and did not help with housework.

✓ Having your **"Day in Court"** is not always what it's cracked up to be. In fact, your insistence on "letting a Judge decide" can be your undoing. When you do go to the courthouse, you may be very disappointed to see a crowded court room full of litigants when your case is scheduled. You might not meet the Judge for months, if ever. Unlike what you see on television, or in the movies, **there is no such thing as an Insta-Divorce**.

✓ The Judge often hears only **"He said" and "She said"** and presumes that both parties (and their lawyers) are stretching the truth, if not outright lying. The Judge is trained to be impartial and objective, which often results in the inevitable conclusion that both sides have contributed to the conflict. Too often, the Judge is simply uninterested in the emotional backstory that fuels every case. **The Judge is also likely thinking**: *"You chose this person as your bride/ groom, and then you chose to start a family together. You stayed with this person for years while he or she did X, Y and/or Z. Don't blame it on the court system if it takes time (i.e. years) to fix the mess you both created."*

Love is Grand. Divorce is a Hundred Grand.
-- Shinichi Suzuki

✓ The adversarial process is **emotionally draining,** and it requires sheer psychological fortitude to endure. Often, a client's sense of normal is skewed. Litigation, whether regarding custody issues or financial claims, can resemble a high stakes game of

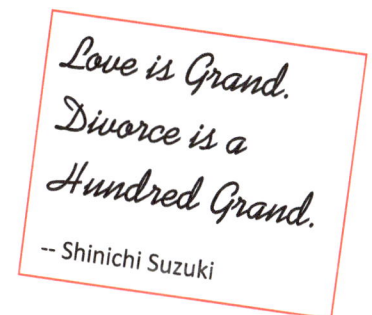

"chicken" or bluffing game. Who will give in first? Who will go broke first paying their lawyer? Who is willing to go all the way to trial? The antagonistic process can lead to permanent embitterment and lifelong enmity between spouses. The lawyers and judges get to go home at the end of the trial. You are left to raise your children with someone that you denigrated in public, and now hate with all your heart.

✓ The mounting legal fees, accounting and appraisal fees, forensic valuation and other litigation fees, not to mention the uncertainty of the ultimate outcome at trial usually provides a strong incentive to settle at some point in the process. **In New York and most other states, over 95% of cases settle before trial.** Prior to trial, the discovery process can cost tens of thousands of dollars, and yield disappointing results. Don't get mad at your lawyer about the court rules and procedural requirements of our judicial system. It's not his or her fault. Remember: The law is the law, and it is what it is.

✓ The cost of a contested divorce proceeding can carry a jaw dropping price tag of $50,000 – $500,000 or more. Many litigants go bankrupt as they hold out for the trial in their divorce case, which can take years. Wouldn't that money be better spent elsewhere? In most cases, **litigation is rarely your only option**, but it is almost always the most costly route. Any opportunity for settlement should be explored, or else you may reach the point where there is no way to go back to the bargaining table. Reread The Smart Split Solution (Chapter 5) for more tips.

✓ One of the risks of going to trial is that even a victory (i.e. a favorable decision by the court) can be an **empty victory**. This is because the losing side can file an appeal, causing even more years of continued turbocharged litigation, stress and tremendous expense. One of the most significant benefits of settling your case is that it completely eliminates the risk of appeal (a/k/a more legal fees).

> *The loser leaves angry and without accepting the result.*
> -- Maimonides (Mishnah Torah)

✓ When will your case finally end? If your case is one of the 95% of cases that settle before trial, your settlement will occur when **you and your spouse are finally able to reach a compromise.** If both you and your spouse walk away from the final settlement, each a little unhappy, then it is probably a fair deal. Take it and move on. Don't look back. The rest of your life is waiting.

CHANGING LAWS OF DIVORCE

It can hardly go unnoticed that the laws of divorce have undergone a major change over the past five years or so[20]. From no-fault divorce grounds (now universally available across the United States), to laws favoring joint custody and those that are gender neutral, not to mention durational maintenance awards, your divorce will not be the same as the one your friend or coworker went through years ago.

The roles of men and women, and societal expectations have changed radically, and this is reflected in the courtroom, and in the laws that are on the books. Most divorce laws today are gender neutral. In an increasing number of households, stay at home fathers are "Mr. Mom", and mothers are the primary breadwinners of the family. In many courtrooms, even SAHM[21] glam housewives and caretakers of small children are directed by the Judge to get back on their feet and go to work at some point. Consequently, most spousal maintenance awards today are rehabilitative in

> *The Judge said, 'All the money', and we'll just shorten it to 'Alimony'.*
> -- Robin Williams

---

[20] Marriage expert Stephanie Coontz has stated that marriage and gender roles have changed more in the past 30 years than in the past 3,000 years.

[21] SAHM = Stay at home mother

nature and limited in duration. In many courtrooms, the standard is moving away from "lifestyle" or "standard of living" and more towards the "reasonable needs" of the dependent spouse. The courts are also more willing than ever to encourage tax advantages to the party paying support.

For all individuals going through the divorce process, it is critical that your expectations match the legal and factual reality. There can be a big price to pay for unreasonable settlement demands – both in court and out of court. No matter how skilled your lawyer is, he or she cannot change the facts of the case, nor the law applied by the Judge. Being smart about your divorce means gaining an understanding about how the law in your jurisdiction applies to the facts of your case. Be aware of the real risks that are created by delaying a settlement. Refusing to settle your case while mindlessly running a tab with your lawyer is a very risky strategy. You might wake up one day wondering why your legal bills are through the roof and why it seems your spouse got the better deal. The absolute worst situation for a client is feeling "forced" to settle, at the eleventh hour before trial, in the hallway outside the courtroom.

> *I try not to think of divorce as failing at marriage, but rather winning at bitterness and resentment.*
> -- Unknown

If you are a dependent spouse, you need to get a crystal clear understanding from your lawyer about the financial support entitlements you can expect. Your lawyer will likely give you a range of possible outcomes, both in terms of duration and the monthly amount. Chances are, the amount and duration of the support you will ultimately be

> *An investment in knowledge pays the best interest.*
> --Ben Franklin

awarded will be less than you think you need. In the words of one of my favorite judges: *"Too bad! So sad!"* Of course, you might worry about your long-term financial security, especially if you are not working. Sooner rather than later, you will need to focus on obtaining full-time employment with medical benefits.

> *The wise course is to profit from the mistakes of others.*
>
> **--Terence**

benefits.   That means it is definitely not too early to brush up your resume and begin looking for a job, even while you are going through the divorce process. Another thing you must do is work with a financial advisor as early as possible to control spending and to build up savings and investments. This is relevant even if you have significant assets from your divorce settlement. Even for those lucky trust funders, if you live beyond your means, your debts will eventually eat up your savings. In the final analysis, you must hold yourself accountable for your financial circumstances and your financial future.

However beautiful the strategy, you should occasionally look at the results.

Winston Churchill

7.

NEXT STEPS

7

PRENUPS AND ESTATE PLANNING ARE NOT JUST FOR MILLIONAIRES

Having a sound financial plan for your family can be the path to peace of mind for yourself. A few decades ago, prenuptial (a/k/a premarital agreements or most commonly, prenups), were used in only rare instances, for the Donald Trumps of the world, or Hollywood celebrities. However, the high divorce rate and the desire to simplify court proceedings have made these agreements more widely used among more segments of society[22]. Another reason for the increase is more people are getting married at an older age. This means they have more wealth coming into the marriage and are more sophisticated about their financial assets.

UNTYING THE KNOT

Simply put, a prenup is a written agreement between two adults about to be married. It is a known fact that engaged couples are more inclined to be fair and reasonable when negotiating financial agreements, whereas divorcing couples are more often motivated by fear

---

[22] However, fewer than 5% of Americans sign a prenup prior to getting hitched.

and loathing and hence, tend not to be reasonable. Most prenups provide for financial matters

if the marriage ends in death or divorce. The prenuptial

agreement overrides the divorce or inheritance laws that

would otherwise apply. It helps to avoid many financial

disputes that occur upon divorce, including spousal

support, who gets the house, even medical insurance.

Instead of getting married again, I'm just going to find a woman I don't like and give her a house. -- Lewis Grizzard

Ideally, the contract protects both spouses in the event the marriage ends. Courts in most

jurisdictions have recognized a strong public policy favoring written agreements that are made

knowingly and in good faith; in virtually all states, a duly executed prenuptial agreement is valid

and enforceable. A party challenging the validity of a prenuptial agreement has the burden of

proof to show that the agreement was the product of fraud, duress, overreaching, or other

misconduct. You must check with a lawyer in your state to find out what specific rules, if any

apply to your situation.

In my law practice, I regularly draft these agreements in cases dealing with a family

business, or a house owned before the marriage. In a recent case, I represented an aspiring

actress who sought to protect her future earnings in the entertainment industry. As you might

expect given the improved financial status of women, I have done many prenups where the

I'll tell you what divorce hasn't taught me. It didn't teach me to not get married again. -- Salman Rushdie

bride-to-be is the monied spouse. Without a prenup, any

financial asset or claim is on the table if there is a break up.

As I have stated before, a contested divorce proceeding can

last for years and can cost hundreds of thousands of dollars.

A prenup is the only legal device that is tantamount to divorce "insurance".

WILL THE PRENUP HOLD UP?

Many clients want assurances that the prenup will hold up in court years later when there is a divorce. There are certain safeguards that should be in place for a 'bullet proof' prenup. Let's review them, shall we?

1. **NO COERCION:** A prenup should be discussed and finalized well before the wedding day.

2. **DISCLOSURE IS REQUIRED:** The parties to the prenup must be up front about all of their assets and income. A prenup can be set aside if there is fraud, nondisclosure or misrepresentation about the income or assets of a party.

3. **EQUAL PLAYING FIELD**: The bride and groom should each have their own lawyer, and have the opportunity to consult with counsel. A good prenup is fair and will address the concerns of both parties, and hopefully, smooth the way for a beautiful wedding and "happily ever after".

Many people who consult with me have preconceived notions about prenups. The very idea of one makes them uncomfortable and defensive. They erroneously assume that these agreements are used only to protect wealthy men from gold diggers. True, prenups are not the most romantic part of wedding planning. Despite the statistical realities regarding divorce, when a couple is in love, the end of the marriage is unthinkable. It can be an awkward conversation to have. However, having candid discussions about financial contributions, expectations and goals *before* getting married is beneficial to the relationship. Where there is a wide disparity in net worth and income, most attorneys agree that a prenup is the way to go.

Other circumstances where prenups are generally advisable are:

When one party has children from a prior marriage or relationship;

When one party expects a large inheritance during the marriage;

When there is a family business or real estate holdings;

When one party is not working and will need support, or has debts;

When there is a concern about social media, privacy or confidentiality;

When the parties have a concern about future compliance with the Jewish Get;

When the parties want to agree on the use of frozen embryos.

"I'm sorry, dear. I wasn't listening. Could you repeat what you've said since we've been married?"

BASIC ESTATE PLANNING

Having a basic estate plan is another important safeguard when you are going through a major life transition, such as a marriage or divorce. The number one protection is to have *a WILL,* the cornerstone of estate planning which will allow you to state your intentions when it comes to who inherits your money, and who financially provides for your children if they are under age 18. A basic Will is inexpensive, and can be prepared in a few hours. Amazingly, about 60% of Americans do not have a Will.

The next important estate planning device is *a LIVING TRUST.* If you put your assets in a living trust, you can retain control of your assets during your lifetime, and get an estate tax benefit for your heirs. After your death, funds will be distributed according to the instructions in your trust. A trust can protect your assets from your ex-spouse, creditors, and even your children.

Next, obtain *a DURABLE POWER OF ATTORNEY* and a *HEALTH CARE PROXY.* These documents designate someone to make financial and medical decisions for you while you are still alive. These documents are very simple to prepare and are relatively inexpensive.

Finally, obtain *LIFE INSURANCE.* If you go through a separation or divorce, you might want to get insurance on your former spouse, to secure your spousal support and/or child support. Life insurance can also be obtained to secure your share of your spouse's retirement assets. Even if you are married, some pensions and retirement plans do not have a death benefit (also called a survivor benefit), so life insurance can be used to replace that source of retirement income.

FINDING *INSPIRATION*

The end of a marriage can be incredibly painful and there is no getting around that. But

I can tell you, having helped thousands of clients get to the end of the process, that divorce will

not destroy you. It's not the end. In fact, it can be a new beginning, allowing you to tap into all

kinds of new possibilities. For many of my clients, divorce starts out as "OMG!" and ends with

"Thank God". Divorce means change – some good, and some bad. You might have to sell or downsize your house or fire the housekeeper. You might have to let go of some 'essential' items in your budget, like a pricey gym membership, or seek paid employment for the first time in many years. Some of these changes can propel you to reclaim your life, to

> *People say, "Oh God, how devastating to go through a divorce!" Did I wish for this to happen to my family? No. But everyone is healthy, we're moving on with our lives.* -- Heidi Klum

remake your life and flourish. Divorce is an opportunity to experience personal growth and to

live a life that really matters according to your own priorities. Work on forgiveness in your

relationships and letting go of emotional baggage. Even if you suffer a personal or financial

setback, you can stand up and be transformed for the better with a newly defined self. Once

you move past the loss, you can and will redefine your future. You deserve to be excited and

fulfilled about what's next in your life, don't you agree?

More than ever, it is critical that you take care of yourself. Pay attention to your sleep

habits, maintain a proper diet and get regular exercise. Spend time with positive people that

will uplift you, not bring you down. **Fasten your eyes on the light at the end of the tunnel.**

Seek out new connections at your church or synagogue, or at the gym. Face to face social connections may be more meaningful than those found online.   Before you embark on a new romance tryst or relationship, consider a few sessions with a therapist. Own up to your own imperfections, and your role in your past relationships, so you don't make the same mistakes again.

If you have children, make them a priority. It is never too late to become a better, more involved parent. More than ever, your children need you to be present in their life, and they need you to be stable and secure in your new life going forward. If you are confident about the path you are on, your children will reflect that confidence. By contrast, if you are in panic and chaos mode, your children will surely show signs of distress. Be the role model your children deserve by showing them how to live a post-divorce life with **Civility, Clarity, and Common Sense.**

FOCUSING ON THE BIG PICTURE

It is very common for clients to feel overwhelmed by the emotional and financial burdens of their case. The experience can feel endless, and clients expect their lawyers and the court system to fix the situation within a certain timeline, for an affordable cost. For many clients, the sense that the case is "almost over" or even making progress is an illusion, due to the absence of tangible results. No settlement is final and binding until there is an agreement signed by both sides, no matter how much time and money has been spent trying to resolve issues. What can you do when you feel hopeless and powerless? Remember: This divorce is a *temporary* stage of your life's journey. *It is not your whole life.* No divorce lasts forever –

although it just might feel that way. You must put the process in perspective and not allow it to take over your life 24/7. Cooperate with your attorney, abide by court orders and legal requirements. Keep an open mind about how you can resolve issues. But other than that, **live your life.** Do not allow the divorce process to define you or consume you. Go out there and be the best parent you can be. Be the best student, friend, boss, and employee you can be. Do not put your "real" life on hold.

<h2 style="text-align:center; color:green;">HANG IN THERE</h2>

The final thoughts I would like to leave you with are these: You <u>will</u> get through this. **Your case will end someday, I promise**. Although divorce is a transformative and life changing experience that can cause tremendous pain and upheaval, it will <u>not</u> break you. Don't dwell on the injustices of the past. Seek help if you need it, and above all, make your decisions from a rational, not emotional place. I wish you peace and well-being in the next chapter of your life.

19 QUOTES TO HELP
SEE YOU THROUGH

....

*"Put one foot in front of the other. The past falls away in every moment.
Keep moving forward."*

....

"One day you will be at the place you always wanted to be."

....

"When you let go, you're creating space for something better."

....

"It's okay not to be okay all of the time."

....

"Sometimes, it's better to keep your cool, remain silent, and smile."

....

....

"Peace, by all means necessary."

....

*"Second chances are often the miracle
we've been waiting for."*

....

"Little by little. Day by day."

....

*"Smile and show everyone you are
stronger than they think."*

....

*"Don't stress. Everything will be okay.
Just let it go."*

....

*"This is the part when you find out
who you are."*

....

"Breathe. It's just a bad day, not a bad life."

....

"Just when the caterpillar thought the world was over, she became a butterfly."

....

"At any given moment, you have the power to say: this is not how the story is going to end."

....

"The only way out is through."

....

"Soon, when all is well, you're going to look back on this period in your life and be so glad that you didn't give up."

....

"Be selective in your battles. Sometimes peace is better than being right."

....

"Karma is real. Let the universe take care of your ex. You can let go."

....

"New day. New start. New opportunities."

....

REALITY-CHECK

EXERCISE #1

Now, it's time for you to write down your favorite quotes. Make these your *positivity mantras* and memorize them. Even better, store these into your smart phone, and set up a daily alert so that you receive a reminder once a day or even throughout the day.

Once this becomes a daily habit, these mantras will become your new truth, which will help you rewire your thoughts, overcome your fears, and move towards a healthier, more positive mindset.

1.

2.

3.

4.

5.

TAKE AWAY STRATEGIES
FOR THE NEW NORMAL

1. Avoid conflict with your ex at all costs, especially if you have children together.

    Indeed, avoiding conflict whenever possible is the secret sauce to a more peaceful post-divorce life.

2. Successful co-parenting requires communication and civility. Make it a habit to share information about your children on a regular basis, including photos, a good score on a math test, and other issues of concern.   Be the catalyst for good (be a positivity Ninja!), even if your ex is not quite on board. Make civility a habit, and show your ex that you will put your children first at all times.

3. If you and your ex are following a regular schedule of parenting time, you might find yourself with a lot of free time on alternate weekends or weekday evenings.   Use it to your advantage. Reconnect with old friends. Make new ones. Pick up new hobbies and new interests that will uplift you.

    > *E. T. began with me trying to write a story about my parents' divorce.*
    > -- Steven Spielberg

4. Plan fun outings for your weekends with your children.

    Schedule a day trip or mini vacation, so that you and your children have something to look forward to on the calendar. Start new family traditions with your children, such as Thursday pizza night, or a hike on Saturday mornings.

5. If you are restarting a career or job search, attend business networking events. You will meet new people, and find new opportunities.

6. Reconnect with your faith. Attend church or synagogue on a more regular basis, and take your children. A spiritual renaissance can work wonders in healing emotional scar tissue.

7. Write in a gratitude journal on a consistent basis. Count your blessings, big and small.

8. After you separate from your ex, clean out your closets and redecorate your living space. Give away unwanted items to charity. You will see a significant psychological benefit by reducing the clutter around you and starting fresh.

> *After my divorce, painting took me out of panic mode and into a serene, calm place. I could absolutely lose myself.* -- Jane Seymour

9. As you simplify your life, make a commitment to reducing debt and increasing savings. Eliminate nonessential expenses. Contribute to a college savings account for your children. Remember, it is never too late to start better financial habits.

10. Encourage your children to start good financial habits as well. Consider paying them a small allowance if they help you with chores. Win-win!

11. When you are ready, join the dating scene, online or elsewhere. But avoid the bad habits and bad relationships of your past. Learn from your past mistakes. And while you're at it, be a goal digger, not a gold digger.

12. To reduce stress, pay attention to your health, including sleep, diet and exercise, which will build up your psychological and emotional infrastructure, not to mention improve your overall physical well being.

REALITY-CHECK **EXERCISE #2**

Name 4 things you can do *today* to improve your outlook:

To relax, I can _____.

To feel good, I can _____.

To reduce stress, I can _____.

I feel peace when I go to _____.

Here is what I am looking forward to in my post-divorce life:

_____

_____

_____

"There is nothing either good or bad, but thinking makes it so." -- Hamlet

8.

RESOURCES

GLOSSARY OF IMPORTANT TERMS[23]

A

Acknowledgment: A formal statement made in front of a notary public, who signs a document and confirms that the signature is authentic.

Action: A lawsuit taken to court.

Addendum: An additional document or phrase attached to the original document.

Affidavit of Service: A document signed by a non-party who has served any papers in a lawsuit such as the Summons and Verified Complaint containing an oath that the papers were properly served. When completed, it is submitted with these papers. Note: One party cannot serve another. This sworn statement must give the date, time, place, the way it was served, and a description of the person who is given the documents.

Agreement: A formal written understanding between two people concerning their respective rights and their duties to each other. (Also referred to as a Stipulation.)

Alternative Dispute Resolution: (ADR) refers to a variety of processes that help parties resolve disputes without a trial. Typical ADR processes for divorce include mediation, neutral evaluation, and collaborative law. These processes are generally confidential, less formal, and less stressful than traditional court proceedings.

Ancillary Relief: In an action for divorce, additional or other help asked for beyond a judgment of divorce, such as maintenance (formerly called "alimony" in New York) payments, division of

---

property, responsibility for debts (bills), child support, etc. (See Equitable Distribution, Maintenance, Marital Property)

Annulment: A court declaration that states that a marriage was never legally valid. After an annulment, the parties are free to remarry.

Answer: The response to the complaint. In a divorce action, the answer must be verified. (See Verified)

Arrears: The unpaid portion of a child support or spousal support order.

Attachment: Seizure of a debtor's property by order of the court. The court takes the property of someone who owes money to another to whom a debt is owed.

Attorney for Child: An attorney appointed by the court to represent a child in contested custody matters (in New York, formerly known as a Law Guardian).

B

Burden of Proof: A party's duty to prove the truth of his or her claims (charges against someone else) in the lawsuit.

C

Calendar Number: The number assigned to a lawsuit by the court when the case is scheduled for trial by the court. It is different from the Index Number that is assigned when the first papers are filed with the County Clerk. A separate fee is charged for the Calendar Number. (See Note of Issue)

Caption: The title of a pleading, motion, or other court filing showing the names of the Plaintiff and Defendant, the name of the court, the court part and the Index or Docket Number.

Cause of Action: A group of facts giving rise to one or more legal reasons for suing; a factual situation that entitles one person to obtain a decision from the court against the other person if proven in court.

Change of Venue: The transfer of a lawsuit from one county to another.

Child Support: Money paid by one parent to another for a child's expenses after separation and/or divorce.

Clerk: A court official who handles filings, motions, pleadings, etc.

Cohabit: To live with, and usually have sexual or romantic relations with, another adult person.

Collaborative Law: Process in which couple hire specially-trained lawyers and other professionals who work to help them resolve their conflict out of court.

Commingle: When one mixes separate funds or properties into a common fund or bank account.

Complaint: The initial pleading to a court in a civil matter, written by the Plaintiff or his/her attorney. In a divorce action, it contains the Plaintiff's allegations of his or her grounds for divorce, and it must be verified. (See Verified, See also Summons)

Contempt: The willful disregard and disrespect of a court order of the judge's authority. Conduct that defies the authority or dignity of a court. It is usually punishable by fine or prison or both.

Contested Divorce: A divorce action which is opposed.

Corroborate: To prove a statement, argument, etc. with confirming facts or evidence.

Counterclaim: A claim by the Defendant against the Plaintiff written in the Verified Answer. A Verified Answer responds only to the allegations (charges) in the Verified Complaint. A counterclaim may be added to the Verified Answer to say that the Defendant also wants a divorce from the Plaintiff and states Defendant's grounds for the divorce.

County Clerk's Office: The office wherein an Index Number and Calendar Number for court proceedings are obtained, court filing fees are paid and court papers are filed and permanently maintained. In many counties, this office is located in the same building as the Supreme Court. If not, the Clerk in the Supreme Court building can direct you to the County Clerk's office.

Custody, Legal: The legal right to make major decisions affecting a child under the age of 18.

Custody, Physical: The actual physical care and control of a child under the age of 18. The person with physical custody usually provides the child's primary residence. Physical custody may also be referred to as Primary Custody or Residential Custody.

D

Default Judgment: A divorce judgment that is obtained against the Defendant when the Defendant fails to respond within the time allowed by law.

Defendant: The person against whom (the person who is served) the divorce action is brought.

Deposition: A person's out-of-court, sworn testimony that is reduced to writing (usually by a court reporter) for later use in the lawsuit. Except for a judge not being present, it is conducted in a manner similar to trial. In New York, also known as an Examination Before Trial (EBT).

Discontinuance: A voluntary ending of a lawsuit.

Discovery: Required disclosure, at a party's request, of information that relates to the litigation. In divorce cases, it usually relates to financial information.

Dissipation: The wasteful use of an asset for an illegal or inequitable purpose, such as a spouse's use of marital property for personal benefit when a divorce is imminent. It is intended to deprive the other spouse of the use and enjoyment of the asset.

Divorce: The legal ending of the marriage between two spouses so that each is free to marry again.

E

Earning Capacity: A person's ability or power to earn money, given the person's talent, skills, training and experience.

Emancipation: The release of a child from the responsibility and control of a parent or guardian. Under New York law, child support must be paid until the age 21. If a child marries, enters the military or becomes self-supporting, before turning 21, the court may consider the child emancipated, and child support may be terminated.

Enjoin: To legally prohibit or restrain by a court injunction (order).

Equitable Distribution: The way marital property must be divided by law in a divorce action in New York State. Equitable distribution does not necessarily mean 50% of one asset to one party and 50% to the other. Distribution is based on various factors presented to the court.

Evidence: Something (including testimony, documents and tangible objects) that tends to prove or disprove the existence of an alleged fact.

Exhibit: A document, record, or other tangible object formally introduced as evidence in court.

Ex Parte (Communication): An application or statement made to the court by one party (including counsel) to a proceeding without notice to, or in the absence of, the other party. This type of communication to the court is generally prohibited, except for scheduling issues.

Expert: A person who, through education or experience, has developed skills or knowledge of a particular subject, so that he or she may form an opinion that will assist the judge or jury in making a decision.

F

Family Court: The Family Court in New York State has the jurisdiction to hear cases involving child support, custody, visitation, spousal support and family offenses (orders of protection). A divorce action cannot be filed in Family Court in New York.

Fiduciary: One who must use a high standard of care in managing another's money or property.

Finding of Fact: A determination by a judge or jury of a fact as proved by the evidence in the record, usually presented at the trial or hearing.

Forensic: Used in courts of law. It relates to the application of a particular subject of expertise such as medicine, science or accounting to the law. In divorce matters, forensics are used to trace assets, value businesses, and evaluate custody issues.

G

Good Faith: Honesty of intention; absence of intent to defraud.

Grounds: Legally sufficient reason for granting of divorce in Supreme Court.

Guardian ad litem: A guardian, usually a lawyer, appointed by the court to help a minor or incompetent person in a lawsuit. In a New York divorce case, the guardian ad litem does not act as an attorney for the child, but reports to the court on what is in the child's best interests.

H

Hearsay: Testimony that is given by a witness who tells not what he or she knows personally, but what others have said which is therefore dependent on the credibility of someone other than the witness. That testimony is generally inadmissible under the rules of evidence.

I

In Camera Inspection: A trial judge's private consideration of evidence. Typically, sensitive information about child custody or business records are reviewed in camera, not in open court.

Index Number: The unique number assigned by the County Clerk's office to every action or proceeding commenced within the New York State Supreme Court. The number is used to identify a case in that court, and should be indicated on all papers served on the parties and filed with the court. The number is either: (a) purchased; or (b) obtained after a Poor Person Application is filed and approved by the court.

Interrogatory: A written question or a set of questions given to the other party in a lawsuit as part of discovery.

Irretrievable Breakdown: the relationship is impossible to repair for a period of at least six months. This is the terminology used for a New York "No Fault" divorce.

J

Judgment of Divorce: A document signed by the court granting the divorce. Depending on which county the case is filed in, in New York, it generally takes between 3 and 6 months to get a final decree of divorce (after the signed settlement agreement and other required documents are filed with the Court.)

Jurisdiction: The authority of a court to act in particular matters.

L

Law Guardian: (see also Attorney for Child and Guardian ad Litem).

M

Maintenance: Spousal support, formerly known as "alimony" in New York.

Marital Property: Any property, regardless of which person is named as owner, that the Plaintiff or Defendant obtained from the date of marriage to the beginning of the divorce action. A house, car, IRA, bank account(s), pension, annuity, business and advanced degree are all examples of marital property. However, an inheritance, a gift from someone other than your spouse, compensation for personal injuries, may be deemed separate property. (See Separate Property)

Mediation: A neutral person called a "mediator" helps the parties try to reach a mutually-acceptable resolution of the dispute. The mediator does not decide the case, but helps the parties communicate so they can try to settle the dispute themselves. Mediation may be inappropriate if a party has a significant advantage in power or control over the other. See Chapter 4 for more information about divorce processes such as Mediation.

N

Nesting (Bird's Nest) Custody: A child centered co-parenting arrangement where the children remain in the family home and the parents take turns moving in and out of the home. It can be a temporary or permanent arrangement, and it is believed to promote the stability and routine of the children.

Notice of Entry: A form given to a party saying that the final judgment of divorce was entered in the County Clerk's Office. A copy of the judgment, date-stamped to indicate the filing, is also given to the party with this document. The time to file a Notice on Appeal commences upon service of the judgment of divorce with Notice of Entry.

Note of Issue: A form filed with the court to notify the court that all documents are ready for the court's review or that the action is ready for trial. A separate fee is charged for filing and a Calendar Number is issued.

O

Order: A direction of the court. Failure to comply may result in an order of contempt, which carries the risk of incarceration and other penalties. (See Contempt)

Order of Protection: An order issued by a court which directs one person to stop certain conduct, such as harassment, against another person. The order may also direct the person to be excluded from the residence and to stay away from the other person, his or her home, school, place of employment and his or her children.

P

Parental alienation is a serious issue that arises in child custody disputes. It occurs when a minor child is manipulated (either directly or indirectly) by one parent to turn away from the other. If there is a rift in the relationship between a parent and child, without any rational explanation, strong action must be taken through the courts to intervene so that the alienation does not get worse.

Party or Parties: A Plaintiff or Defendant in a legal proceeding.

Plaintiff: The person who starts the divorce action/lawsuit.

Poor Person Application: An application made to the court in New York, by either the Plaintiff or Defendant, stating that because of insufficient income he or she is unable to pay the court fees normally required for divorce actions. If the application is granted by the court, the usual court costs for the divorce action are waived.

Prenuptial Agreement (Prenup): A written contract between two people who are about to marry addressing assets, spousal support, future earnings and division of property. The contract is binding upon death of a party or divorce. A postnuptial agreement (Postnup) is the same as a prenuptial agreement, except that it is signed after the wedding.

Pro Se: (Self-Represented) Appearing on one's own behalf without an attorney.

Q

QDRO: Qualified Domestic Relations Order. An order signed by the court stating what portion of one spouse's pension is to be awarded to the other spouse.

R

Removal of Barriers to Remarriage Form: In New York, this form is necessary when the marriage was solemnized in a religious ceremony by a member of the clergy, minister of any religion, or a leader of The Society for Ethical Culture. It requires the party obtaining the divorce to acknowledge that he or she has taken all steps to remove religious barriers to the other party's remarriage. This specifically pertains to the Jewish "Get".

Request for Judicial Intervention (RJI): A form filed with the New York court to request to have a judge assigned to the case.

S

Separate Property: Property considered by the courts to belong only to one spouse or the other. If the court decrees that certain assets are separate property of one party, then those assets are not divided between the parties as marital property.

Separation: One spouse's absence from the marital household prior to divorce.

Separation Agreement: A written agreement on support for the child or children, spousal maintenance payments, division of marital property, responsibility for debts (bills), custodial residence of minor children, child care and related issues. In New York, this agreement must be formally signed and acknowledged and covers the period before divorce but after the separation. (See Acknowledgment).

Service: Formal delivery of a legal paper such as delivery of a Writ, Summons with Notice, or Summons and Verified Complaint officially notifying the recipient that he or she is a party in a lawsuit.

Settlement Agreement: A formal, voluntary, written agreement on all of the issues surrounding divorce. It must be formally signed and acknowledged. (See Acknowledgment).

Spouse: Husband or wife.

Statute of Limitations: The time limit in which to bring an action.

Stipulation: A voluntary agreement between parties on an issue or issues related to the divorce proceedings. Also referred to as an Agreement.

Subpoena: A legal order requiring a person's attendance at a particular time and place to testify as a witness or to provide certain documents that are requested. Failure to comply can result in contempt of court order. (Also known as a Judicial Subpoena)

Summons with Notice: In New York, a legal document which starts the Plaintiff's action for a divorce and requires the Defendant to serve a Notice of Appearance in the action within a specific period of time. This document is initially filed with the County Clerk's Office and a copy is then served upon the Defendant to give notice that the Plaintiff has started a divorce action. It states the grounds for the divorce and may also include requests for additional relief such as: child support, custody, visitation, spousal maintenance and equitable distribution.

Support: Payment for housing, food, clothing, and related living expenses.

Supreme Court: The highest trial-level court in New York State. Divorce actions may be started only in this court. Appeals of Supreme Court orders and Family Court orders go to the Appellate Division.

Supreme Court Clerk's Office: An office, separate from the County Clerk's Office, which provides clerical support to the Supreme Court.

T

Third Party: A party to a court action who is not the Plaintiff or Defendant.

U

Unemancipated or Minor Children: Children under the age of 21 who are supported by a parent or guardian. (See Emancipation)

Uncontested Divorce: An uncontested divorce occurs when: (a) there are no disagreements between you and your spouse over any financial or divorce-related issues (i.e., child custody and support, division of marital property or spousal support); and (b) your spouse either agrees to the divorce, or fails to appear in the divorce action.

V

Venue: The permissible place for the trial of a lawsuit.

Verified: Sworn before a notary public that the facts made in that document are true. Most pleadings in a matrimonial action must be verified. (See also Acknowledgment; Answer; Complaint).

Visitation: The right of a non-custodial parent to be with a child. Also referred to as Parenting Time.

W

Waiver: Knowingly, intentionally giving up rights or claims.

Writ: (Also Writ of Habeas Corpus) A legal order signed by a judge directing that a person (generally a child in divorce cases) be brought before the court.

A CHILD'S BILL OF RIGHTS

Many matrimonial attorneys, mediators, and therapists are familiar with this Bill of Rights, or a similar version. Bottom line: Your children didn't ask for their lives to be turned upside down. They didn't ask for their relationship to one or both of their parents to be compromised. Your children have the right to know and love both of their parents, notwithstanding all of the negative emotions running between the adults in their lives. Despite the challenges, parents must do their part to ensure that their children are subjected to a minimal level of upheaval in their lives. After all, parents who truly are seeking the best interests of their children should respect these basic rights, don't you agree?

Every child whose parents get divorced has:

1. The right to love and be loved by both of parents without feeling guilt or disapproval.

2. The right to be protected from each parent's anger with each other.

3. The right to be kept out of the middle of parental conflict, including the right not to pick sides, carry messages, or hear complaints about the other parent.

4. The right to know well in advance about important changes that will affect the child's life; for example, when one of the parents is going to move or get remarried.

5. The right to reasonable financial support during childhood and through the college years, from both parents.

6. The right to have feelings, to express feelings, and to have both parents listen.

7. The right to have a life that is a close as possible to what it would have been if the parents stayed together.

8. **The right to** reasonable use of the telephone to place and receive calls with the other parent and relatives.

9. The right to be shielded from derogatory remarks about the other parent to the child, or engage in abusive, coarse or foul language, which can be overheard by the child.

10. The right to be shielded from hearing arguments, negotiations, or other substantive discussions about legal or financial matters between the parents, including child support issues.

11. The right to an acknowledgment from both parents that the child has two homes, although the child may spend more time at one home than the other.

12. The right not to be interrogated about the other parent or what goes on in the other parent's household.

13. The right to be transported at all times by a person who is not impaired due to consumption of alcohol or illegal drugs.

"Before you decide which parent to live with, look who's hanging out on my street, Bobby."

Contested Divorce Timeline

If your case goes to court in New York, it will follow the steps outlined below[24].

RJI Filed

A Request for Judicial Intervention (RJI) must be filed no later than 45 days from service of the Summons for Divorce.

OR

A Request for Judicial Intervention (RJI) must be filed no later than 120 days from service of the summons if a Notice of No Necessity is filed by both parties.

STATEMENT OF NET WORTH

A Statement of Net Worth (sworn financial affidavit listed your assets, debts, income and expenses) must be exchanged between the parties and filed no later than 10 days prior to the preliminary conference (your first court date).

Refer to NYCRR § 202.16(f)(1) for other papers which the court directs to be exchanged.

PRELIMINARY CONFERENCE

A preliminary conference must be held within 45 days of judicial assignment

(RJI filing date).

NOTE: Both parties must be present, and the judge shall address the parties.

---

[24] Adapted from NYcourts.gov

COMPLIANCE CONFERENCE

A compliance conference shall be scheduled unless the court dispenses with it based upon a stipulation of compliance filed by the parties. At the compliance conference, issues regarding discovery, financial disclosure, and interim support and custody issues are usually dealt with.

Before the case goes to trial, there are usually at least three compliance conferences.

NOTE: Parties must be present unless otherwise advised by the court, and the judge shall address the parties.

DISCOVERY

Discovery (encompasses all financial disclosure, depositions, production of documents, valuation of businesses and appraisals of assets) shall be completed and a Note of Issue filed no later than 6 months from the date the preliminary conference was held unless otherwise shortened or extended by the court dependent upon the circumstances.

TRIAL

A trial shall be scheduled no later than 6 months from the date the preliminary conference was held.   Trial is scheduled after all discovery is completed.

ABOUT THE AUTHOR

Jacqueline Harounian, Esq is a partner at the Law Firm of Wisselman, Harounian & Associates, PC in Great Neck, New York and a recognized leader in the field of matrimonial and family law. She skillfully and adeptly handles complex divorce, custody and support matters in the Family and Supreme Courts on Long Island and the five boroughs of New York City. As a highly experienced trial attorney, Jackie nevertheless believes that a negotiated settlement, rather than litigation, is the preferred strategy for her clients. Her approach is client focused, straightforward and empathetic. She provides respect and compassion, guiding her clients towards a cost effective and clear-cut resolution that is in their best interest.

Jackie attended Columbia College (B.A. *cum laude*, English Literature and Middle Eastern Languages) and thereafter, Hofstra University School of Law (J.D. *with honors).* She was admitted to practice law in New York State, 2nd Department, in 1995, and admitted to practice before The Supreme Court of the United States in 2013. Among her many accolades, she is rated "Pre Eminent" and recognized with the highest possible peer review rating ("AV") by Martindale-Hubbell for legal ability and professional ethics, with a "Superb" rating (10 out of 10) on Avvo.com. She has been chosen to the Super Lawyers list for the past six consecutive years (2010-2015), and Super Lawyers has repeatedly selected her as one of the "Top 50 Women Lawyers" in New York, each time as the only Long Island divorce attorney on the list.

Public service and volunteering have always been a priority for Jackie since she began her legal career. She is the current President of Yashar, the Attorneys and Lawyers Chapter of Hadassah. Since 2007, she has been an Adjunct Professor of Family Law at Hofstra Law School. She lectures on a regular basis to attorneys, accountants, mental health professionals, police departments, and bar associations. She is a sought after speaker for a range of topics including financial and legal empowerment, negotiating skills, and women's issues. She has been involved in efforts to advance legislation in her field, including same sex marriage laws, and proposed child abduction legislation. Jackie has made numerous television appearances as an expert in family law, including WABC Good Morning America; WCBS Evening News, radio and cable programs. Her advice is featured on a regular basis in print media, including Newsweek, The New York Times, and The Huffington Post. Connect with Jackie at www.divorcercalitycheck.com.

ACKNOWLEDGMENTS

It is the most wonderful irony that despite my chosen field of practice, I have been blessed with a long marriage at home and at work. Credit goes first to the *uber-mensch:* my spouse of 25+ years, Maurice Harounian, and our four delightful and self-reliant children whom I love beyond measure: Aaron, Tamara, Delilah and Joey. I am immensely grateful to my second family of 20+ years, the dedicated attorneys and staff at The Law Firm of Wisselman, Harounian & Associates, P.C., especially my partner, Jerome Wisselman. Finally, thank you to my earliest role models in life: my parents, Parry and Parviz Yousefzadeh, and my sisters, Janet Esagoff, Esq., and Dr. Edna Ohebshalom.

"She had one helluva good lawyer."

www.ingramcontent.com/pod-product-compliance
Lightning Source LLC
Chambersburg PA
CBHW041444210326
41599CB00004B/128